PAUL A. PORTER

METAPHORS AND MONSTERS

A literary-critical study of Daniel 7 and 8

CWK GLEERUP

Doctoral dissertation at the University of Uppsala, 1983
ISBN 91-40-04867-5

CWK Gleerup is the imprint for the scientific and scholarly publications of
Liber Förlag, Lund

Abstract

Porter, P. A. Metaphors and Monsters. A literary-critical study of Daniel 7 and 8. *Coniectanea Biblica*. *Old Testament* Series 20. xii+128 pp. Uppsala. ISBN 91-40-04867-5

In this study, we examine three interrelated aspects of the animal metaphors of Daniel 7 and 8. These are (1) the identification of the beasts of the visions with various kings in the interpretations (Part I); (2) the physical peculiarities of the beasts in both visions (Part II); and (3) the semantically deviant functional characteristics of the animals in both chapters (Part III).

Application of Max Black's interaction theory of metaphor in Part I alerts us to the semantic importance of the animal images in the immediate linguistic context provided by each vision and its accompanying interpretation. In Part II, we account for the physical peculiarities of the various animals in the light of Mesopotamian birth-omen traditions. Finally, in Part III, comparison of the Daniel visions with 1 Enoch 85–90 and various OT lamentation texts leads us to the conclusion that the root metaphor "shepherd" informs the numerous semantic domains relative to the beasts of Daniel 7 and 8, consequently providing the basis for interactions across these various domains, which in turn account for the functional characteristics of the beasts described.

In all three Parts of the study, we note the semantic importance of the animal metaphors of Daniel 7 and 8, while the identification of birth anomalies with shepherd rulers in Mesopotamian texts and later apocalyptic works enables us to integrate the findings of Parts II and III.

The Maccabean author of Daniel 7 and 8 is viewed as one who turns to earlier Israelite laments to express the anguish and hopes of his own generation. In exilic/post-exilic complaints awaiting eschatological deliverance from gentile rule, he hears a prophetic note addressed to his, the last generation of Israel in "exile." In this way, animal images in these various laments form the basis of his two visions. On the other hand, the author's cosmopolitan interests, which are already indicated in the earlier chapters of Daniel, account for the bizarre anomalous features of the various beasts.

Paul A. Porter. Teologiska institutionen, Uppsala Universitet, Box 2006, S-750 02 Uppsala, Sweden.

Printed in Sweden by
Borgströms Tryckeri AB, Motala 1983

for my desley

Table of Contents

Strange beasts

Of the four visions recorded in the book of Daniel, those in chapters 7 and 8 are perhaps the most important, and certainly the most arresting. Chapter 7, for example, paints a spectacular picture of the great judgment session in which the white-haired Ancient of Days ceremoniously reviews the books of record, smites the wicked oppressor, enthrones the son of man and delivers his verdict in favour of the saints of the Most High. No less awe-inspiring is the vision of the following chapter. Here Daniel returns from the divine council with a promise answering the fondest hopes of his fellow-countrymen: the speedy restoration of the Jerusalem temple (8:14).

These two grand themes—the judgment and the new temple—are not only central to Daniel, but also inform the eschatological hopes of OT, intertestamental and NT writers.

Disconcerting in this regard are the bizarre animals introducing each of the Daniel visions. In order to expound the meaning of judgment and temple, (so it would seem), Daniel first of all escorts his readers through a magic zoo of fearsome and fabulous beasts. This juxtaposition of the sublime with the seemingly ridiculous has bewildered more than one reader, and gives rise to a host of immediate questions: Why should beasts come into judgment, and why anomalous beasts in particular? What, ultimately, does the destiny of the temple have to do with a ram or an ill-tempered he-goat? Again, why are animal horns so obviously important to the author? All told, no fewer than nineteen of them confront the reader: horns with human characteristics, rapidly growing horns, horns that are uprooted, others that are broken, little horns, large horns, horns that seem to multiply, a horn waging war on the saints and a horn that presumes to attack the sanctuary and the stars of heaven. Why should a horn ever do a thing like that? Finally, what rationale led the author of these chapters to identify this exotic menagerie with his neighbouring countries and their respective kings?

Questions of this sort inevitably lead one into the area of metaphor analysis.

For centuries, exegetes of Daniel 7 and 8 regarded the picture-language of these chapters as a decorative substitute for some other literal meaning of a historical, ethical or theological order. Given this common assumption concerning the nature of metaphor, the task of interpreting these images seemed clearly defined: anyone who cared to burrow deeply enough beneath the unsophisticated veneer of these "mere metaphors" might reasonably hope to extract the "real" message of the author. Such, for example, was the common goal of the Historicist, Preterist and Futurist fathers of apocalyptic exegesis, who turned to events in Reformation Europe, Maccabean history and latter-day Jerusalem respectively, for the meaning of Daniel's visions. In the twentieth century, the same assumption has continued virtually unchallenged in numerous studies of apocalyptic.

The reason for this state of affairs is not hard to find. Ever since Aristotle originally defined metaphor as "giving the thing a name that belongs to something else," religious and philosophical thinkers alike have tended to view metaphor as a rhetorical flourish devoid of semantic significance.

In recent years, however, the study of metaphor has become philosophically respectable. Metaphor, long dismissed as frivolous and inessential, is now regarded by most language philosophers and linguists as capable of conveying genuine meaning.

In the field of biblical exegesis, interpreters of the gospel parables have been foremost in exploiting this radical re-estimate of the importance of metaphor. Here it is sufficient to mention the literary-critical studies of Wilder (1964), Funk (1966), Via (1967), Crossan (1973), TeSelle (1975), Ricoeur (1975), Perrin (1976), Weder (1978) and Klauck (1978).

Although symbolic language is particularly pronounced in apocalyptic, exegetes of this literature genre have scarcely begun to explore these texts from the vantage point of modern metaphor theory. Notable exceptions are Collins (1974, 1977, 1981), Ricoeur (1979) and Koch (1983), whose recent studies have underscored the semantic importance of apocalyptic metaphor.

In the present study, we seek to give full rein to the complexity of Daniel's animal metaphors by examining not only the identification of kings with animals in the visionary interpretations (Part I), but also the *physical* peculiarities of the various beasts (Part II) as well as their *functional* characteristics (Part III). In our opinion, these are three interdependent areas of inquiry. To illustrate: whereas to say, "The king of Greece is a he-goat" (cf. Dan 8:21) would be to give utterance to a relatively simple metaphorical expression (cf. the hackneyed example, "Richard is a lion"), the statement becomes considerably more complex when one says, "The king of Greece is a he-goat *with a horn between its eyes, four horns and a little horn*" (cf. Dan 8:5, 8, 9). Expressions of this sort draw attention to the physical peculiarities of the animal concerned. Even more complex is the metaphorical expression, "The king of Greece is a he-goat with a horn between its eyes, four horns, and a little horn *which attacks the stars, the truth and the sanctuary*" (cf. Dan 8:10–13). This statement not only takes into account the identification of beast with king and the physical peculiarities of the beast, but also invites consideration of the animal's semantically deviant functional characteristics. A viable analysis of the animal metaphors of these chapters, we believe, should successfully integrate results accruing from all three areas of inquiry.

Briefly stated, our thesis is that the animal metaphors in their complexity find their roots in the OT and ancient Near Eastern notion of the shepherd king.

Acknowledgements

It is a pleasure to thank the following people for their criticisms and numerous valuable suggestions during the preparation of this study: my supervisor, Prof. Helmer Ringgren, Profs. Lars Hartman and Jan Bergman of Uppsala, and Prof. Klaus Koch of Hamburg.

Dr. António Barbosa da Silva also read the entire manuscript and provided inestimable help in matters pertaining to metaphor analysis.

Several friends and relatives have taken a lively interest in this project, and have assisted generously with financial means. Particular thanks are due to Mic and Marianne Walter, Sandy and Belle Porter, Malcolm and Marie Porter, David and Sylvia Mason, and Arthur and Joyce Markwell.

Finally, my appreciation to Drs. Desmond Ford and John T. Townsend, whose classes in apocalyptic have stimulated my interest in the animal visions of Daniel.

P. A. P.

PART I

''The king of Greece is a he-goat ...''

CHAPTER 1

The semantic importance of the animal images

Introduction

When the author of Daniel 7 and 8 identifies certain kings or nations with the animals of his visions, are these animal images semantically important, or are they merely literary decorations? Answers to this question depend on the particular view or views of metaphor considered appropriate for the analysis of these chapters. In current exegetical discussions, each of the following views is represented:

a. *Metaphor as substitution.* According to this view, the visions are simply codes awaiting decipherment. The sole task of the animal images, therefore, is to provide a substitute for the kings or nations they represent. Other images might have been just as appropriate.[1]

b. *Metaphor as comparison.* Adherents of this view[2] seek to draw certain

---

[1] Cf. Perrin 1974, 11–12: "Let me begin this aspect of my discussion by pointing out that in ancient Jewish apocalyptic in general—and for that matter in early Christian apocalyptic in general—the symbols used are, in Wheelwright's terms, 'steno-symbols'; in Ricoeur's, 'signs' rather than 'symbols.' Typically, the apocalyptic seer told the story of the history of his people in symbols where each symbol bore a one-to-one relationship with that which it depicted. This thing was Antiochus IV Epiphanes, that thing was Judas Maccabee, the other thing was the coming of the Romans, and so on. But if this was the case, and it certainly was, then when the seer left the known facts of the past and present to express his expectation of the future his symbols remained 'steno-symbols', and his expectation concerned singular concrete historical events ... the whole paraphernalia of apocalyptic sign-giving is dependent upon a one-to-one correspondence between the sign/symbol and that which it represents ..." Similarly, Hartman and di Lella 1978, 91, 212, 235: "Since, as is generally agreed, the four hideous beasts in 7:3–7 symbolize only the four pagan empires, 'the little horn' symbolizes Antiochus IV, and the 'Ancient One' (vss. 9, 13, 22) symbolizes the God of Israel, then we must assume that those responsible for this apocalypse meant each of these symbols to have a one-to-one relationship with the respective reality being symbolized. Thus, to coin two new ... terms, unireferential symbols were employed in this chapter, and not multireferential symbols which can have more than a one-to-one relationship." "But essentially the four monstrous beasts of Dan 7:3–7 are ad hoc creations of the author ... for the purpose of symbolizing the four successive kingdoms of men ..." "For our author the one horn and the four horns are mere symbols for one kingdom and four kingdoms, respectively." Cf. also Davies 1980, 47: "While not wishing to comment on whether symbols in Daniel are unireferential or not, it seems to me that many of them are in fact not conscious echoes of imagery drawn from mythology or anywhere else .... When we are able to find similarities between, for example, descriptions of beasts in Daniel and elsewhere, we have in all likelihood reached the limit."

[2] The comparison view is actually a variant of the substitution view. See Black 1962, 35: "It will be noticed that a 'comparison view' is a special case of the 'substitution view.' For it holds that the metaphorical statement might be replaced by an equivalent literal *comparison*."

points of comparison between the various beasts and the corresponding kings or nations. The he-goat represents the king of Greece, for example, because he is in some way *like* the king of Greece, and vice versa.[3] Most exegetes of Daniel 7 and 8 hold a combination of substitution and comparison views.

c. *Metaphor as semantic "tension" or "interaction."*[4] Underlying this approach is the conviction that certain metaphorical expressions in Daniel 7 and 8 are semantically active.[5] Just as new things may emerge in nature from hitherto ungrouped combinations of elements, so tensive or interaction-type metaphorical expressions communicate new meaning by juxtaposing normally unjoined ideas or images.[6] In such instances, "we have two thoughts of different things active together and supported by a single word, or phrase, whose meaning is a resultant of their interaction."[7]

We believe that a tension or interaction view of metaphor is indispensable for a correct understanding of Daniel's animal images. Perhaps the finest modern statement of the interaction view is that developed by the language philosopher Max Black.[8] In the remainder of this chapter, we shall use Black's theory of metaphor to demonstrate the semantic importance of the animal images as visionary symbols.[9]

Black's interaction theory of metaphor

Metaphor and the question of context

According to Black, a word or a phrase receives a metaphorical meaning in a specific context.

---

[3] Cf. Porteous 1979, 105: "The bear as a symbol for the Median kingdom has most probably been chosen because of its known ferocity (see Isa 13:17–18) and the dread it aroused (Isa 21:2ff)." Similarly, Hartman and di Lella, 1978, 234: "The symbolic animals are well chosen; just as a male sheep cannot withstand an attack by a male goat, so the Persian empire was easily overcome by Alexander."

[4] The term "metaphoric tension" has been popularized by Philip Wheelwright (1954, 101–122), whose views in several respects approximate those of I. A. Richards, who advocated an "interaction" view of metaphor (cf. n. 7 below).

[5] Cf. Collins 1977, 114: "The four kings/kingdoms are presented in Daniel 7 as manifestations of the ancient chaos monster. It should be quite clear that we are not dealing here with a code which can be discarded when it is deciphered. We cannot say that the statement in Dan 7:3, 'four great beasts came up out of the sea,' is adequately paraphrased in Dan 7:17, 'these four great beasts are four kings who shall arise out of the earth.'" Cf. also Collins 1974a, 5–27, and Ricoeur, in Lacocque 1979, xxii. Similarly, Koch (1983, 437–440) finds the substitution view of metaphor inadequate for the exegesis of Daniel 8.

[6] Cf. Wheelwright 1962, 85–86.

[7] Richards 1936, 93.

[8] Most recently, Black 1979, 19–43.

[9] See Black 1962, 25–47; 1979, 19–43. Our description of Black's interaction theory is essentially a précis of these two essays.

4

a. *Linguistic context*. Black distinguishes between the linguistic "focus" and "frame" of a metaphorical expression. In the statement, "The chairman ploughed through the discussion," the word "ploughed" contrasts with the remaining words by which it is accompanied. It is, consequently, the focus, and the frame constitutes the remainder of the sentence. The distinction is a semantic one. One frame succeeds in making a word a metaphor, while another frame may fail. On the other hand, the statement, "I like to plough my memories occasionally," (which has the same focus as the previous example), may be regarded as a case of identical metaphor, provided the two frames are considered to be sufficiently alike.

b. *Extralinguistic context*. Frequently, a correct understanding of metaphor can be reconstructed only from its social or extralinguistic context, i.e., the particular circumstances of its utterance, the thoughts, acts, feelings and intentions of the speaker, the tone of voice, the verbal setting and the historical background. Such a context is, in the last resort, an ambiguous one, and just as there is no infallible test for resolving ambiguity, so there is none to be expected in identifying and interpreting metaphorical expressions occurring in this context. A literally true statement might well be metaphorical. When we say, "He does indeed live in a glass house," of a man who actually lives in a house made of glass, nothing prevents us from using the sentence to make a metaphorical statement. Considerations such as these place metaphor analysis ultimately in the domain, not of semantics—the study of meaning—but of pragmatics—the study of speech acts and the extralinguistic contexts in which they occur.[10]

The interaction theory

Black develops the interaction view into a set of claims:

a. A metaphorical statement has two distinct subjects, to be identified as the "primary" subject and the "secondary" one. Thus, if one says, "The poor are the negroes of Europe," "the poor" is the primary subject and "negroes" the secondary one.

b. The secondary subject is to be regarded as a system rather than an individual thing. Thus, in the above example, the presence of the word "negroes" signalizes a system of relationships or "implicative complex," thereby calling into mind numerous ideas, images, sentiments, values and stereotypes.

c. The metaphorical utterance works by "projecting upon" the primary subject a set of "associated implications" comprised in the implicative complex, that are predicable of the secondary subject. In the example cited,

---

[10] Ortony 1979, 5.

5

for instance, "the poor" of Europe might be viewed not merely as an oppressed class, but also as partaking of the inherited and indelible qualities of "natural" poverty attributed to black Americans by white racists.[11]

    d. The implicative complex may consist of deviant implications established *ad hoc* by the author of the metaphor.

    e. In the context of a particular metaphorical statement, the two subjects "interact" in the following ways: (i) the presence of the primary subject incites the hearer to select some of the secondary subject's properties; and (ii) invites him to construct a parallel implicative complex that can fit the primary subject; and (iii) reciprocally induces parallel changes in the secondary subject. Thus, metaphorical expressions may be said to act as "filters." For example, in the sentence, "Man is a wolf," the primary subject, "man," is seen through the filter of the secondary subject, "wolf." Any human traits that can be talked about in "wolf-language" will be rendered prominent, and any that cannot will be pushed into the background. The wolf-metaphor suppresses some details, emphasizes others—in short, organizes our view of man. Another illustration may be taken from the world of chess:

Suppose I am set the task of describing a battle in words drawn as largely as possible from the vocabulary of chess. These latter terms determine a system of implications which will proceed to control my description of the battle. The enforced choice of the chess vocabulary will lead some aspects of the battle to be emphasized, others to be neglected, and all to be organized in a way that would cause much more strain in other modes of description. The chess vocabulary filters and transforms: it not only selects, it brings forward aspects of the battle that might not be seen at all through another medium.[12]

Daniel 7 and 8 and the interaction view

Having briefly outlined Black's theory of metaphor, we shall apply it to Daniel 7 and 8 in the following way:

The question of context

For our present purpose, the two chapters, individually considered, provide the immediate linguistic context or frame for metaphor analysis. Later in the study, we shall examine both chapters as a unit. Although Daniel 7 and 8 represent two self-contained vision reports,[13] beasts and horns feature

---

[11] Turner 1974, 30.
[12] Black 1962, 41–42.
[13] Working with the text as it stands, we assume the unity of each chapter.

6

prominently in both chapters as visionary symbols. Moreover, Daniel 8:1 specifically refers the reader back to the vision of the previous chapter.[14]

Everyone agrees that there are numerous specific parallels with chapter 7 and chapter 8. It is once again partly a question of the same empires, here too represented by horned animals. They make war on the "Saints," but the time of their hegemony is measured. The last enemy will soon be vanquished—Antiochus IV "will be broken without the intervention of any human hand" (v. 24).[15]

Daniel 7 and 8 will also be considered within the broader linguistic context afforded by the book of Daniel as a whole. Whereas Lenglet demonstrated the symmetrical arrangement of the Aramaic chapters 2–7, with chapter 2 corresponding to chapter 7, chapter 3 to chapter 6 and chapter 4 to chapter 5,[16] Collins has shown that, beyond certain motifs shared by chapters 2 and 7 (e.g., the four kingdoms), chapter 7 along with the latter section of the book provides an interpretation of the persecution of Antiochus Epiphanes, which finds no clear mention in chapters 2–6. Consequently, chapter 7 should be grouped with chapters 8–12 rather than with chapters 2–6.[17] Daniel 7, therefore, "serves as a linking chapter by which the two halves of the book are interlocked."[18] Finally, it will be necessary to examine the animal metaphors within the extralinguistic context informing the book of Daniel itself. The historico-cultural background of the book, its place within the broader stream of Jewish apocalyptic tradition, as well as its relation to both OT and ancient Near-Eastern traditions will require consideration in later chapters of this study.

The visions and the interpretations

For the immediate purpose of this chapter, the relation of the visions to the interpretations in Daniel 7 and 8 may be described in the following way:[19]

a. *The symbolic visions.* Whereas to say A (the primary subject) is B (the secondary subject) would be a case of simple metaphor, the symbolic visions speak of B without referring to A, although it is supposed that A, or an A, is intended.[20] Thus, although it is clear from the interpretations that Daniel is chiefly interested in individuals and events in the human rather

---

[14] Dan 8:1: "a vision appeared to me, Daniel after (ʾḥry) that which appeared to me at the first." Cf. Ehrlich 1914, 144–145, who takes ʾḥry to indicate "in the manner of" or "like."
[15] Lacocque 1979, 156.
[16] Lenglet 1972, 169–190.
[17] Collins 1977, 11–14.
[18] Collins 1977, 14.
[19] As will be shown in Chapter Two below, the relation between the visions and the interpretations in Daniel 7 and 8 is more complex. Our present goal is simply to establish the semantic importance of the animal images of the visions.
[20] Cf. Barfield 1947, 107.

than zoological realm, his visions are dominated by animal rather than human imagery. The primary subject (i.e., the referent) is consistently suppressed.

b. *The interpretations*. It is the interpretations which link up primary and secondary subjects in Daniel 7 and 8 (e.g., "The he-goat is the king of Greece"). Such expressions differ from simple metaphorical statements in the following ways: (i) The secondary subject is mentioned before the primary subject—NOT "The king of Greece is the he-goat," BUT "The he-goat is the king of Greece." The secondary subject precedes the primary subject because (ii) The expression is characteristically interpretative.[21] It might equally be rendered as "The he-goat *means* the king of Greece." This, however, raises the semantic problem as to whether we are dealing here with a metaphor at all, since, *at the level of the sentence*, the statement, "The he-goat means the king of Greece" is literal rather than metaphorical. Notwithstanding, *at the level of the discourse* (i.e., vision + interpretation), the author clearly identifies the he-goat with the king of Greece in order to create a metaphor. (iii) The expression is characteristically specific—NOT "*A* he-goat is the king of Greece," BUT "*The* he-goat is the king of Greece." This leads us to the final point: (iv) Interpretative metaphorical expressions may involve secondary subjects which have ready-made or *ad hoc* implicative complexes. Thus, when our author says, "The he-goat is the king of Greece," he is saying, at the level of the discourse, something like this: "The king of Greece is a he-goat. Not just any he-goat, mind you, but specifically the one whose characteristics I have already prescribed in the vision."

Why a tension or interaction view is necessary

Thus far, our discussion of the relation of the visions to the interpretations has remained more or less within the descriptive range of both substitution and comparison views of metaphor. In what follows, we consider those characteristics of the animal metaphors which seem to defy analysis according to either view.

a. *Development and correspondence*. Neither the substitution nor the comparison view successfully accounts for the fact that several details in the visions are totally ignored in the corresponding interpretations.[22] Among such details are some of the most interesting ones: (e.g., in chapter 7: the

---

[21] Cf. Frye 1957, 125: "Finally, identification belongs not only to the structure of poetry, but to the structure of criticism as well, at least of commentary. Interpretation proceeds by metaphor as well as creation, and even more explicitly. When St. Paul interprets the story of Abraham's wives in Genesis, for instance, he says that Hagar 'is' Mount Sinai in Arabia."
[22] Cf. Collins 1977, 114–115.

four winds, the great sea, the wings and man-like features of the lion, the raised side of the bear and the three ribs in its mouth, the wings and four heads of the panther; in chapter 8: the riverbank, the unnamed beasts conquered by the ram, and the peculiar formation of the horns of the ram and the he-goat). Equally striking is the relative lack of space given to the interpretation of these beasts within each chapter. Daniel 7 devotes five verses to describing the first three beasts (vss. 2–6), but only one brief verse (v. 17) to their interpretation. Similarly, whereas chapter 8 requires seven verses to depict the exploits of the ram and he-goat (vss. 2–8), the corresponding interpretation appears in just two verses (vss. 20–21). Both visions, in short, seem to have an evocative power which is not exhausted in the interpretations. The interpretations provide an inadequate substitute for the visions, and also fail to supply sufficient instances of comparison between symbol and referent.

Comparable for its high development and relatively low correspondence is the instance of simile in Song of Songs 4:2:

Your teeth are like a flock of shorn ewes that have come up from the washing, all of which bear twins, and none of them is bereaved.

Here the pastoral image is clearly more important than the young lady's dentistry! Similarly, Daniel 7 and 8 defy description according to substitution and comparison views of metaphor, both of which require specific referents for all or most details of the visions.[23]

b. *Interaction.* We shall now proceed to examine two specific cases of interaction in Daniel 7 and 8. It was noted above that in both visions, the primary subject is assumed but largely suppressed. In each vision, then, the animals constitute the secondary subject, whereas the primary subject belongs to the interpretations. To what extent can primary and secondary subjects be seen to interact in these passages?

Little is achieved if all that can be demonstrated is the influence of the primary subject on the secondary subject, since such a process can be adequately accounted for by substitution and comparison views of metaphor. Compare, for example 1 Enoch 90:19:

---

[23] It might, of course, be argued that the visions naively reproduce well-known complex images (e.g., hybrid Mesopotamian art forms), whose detailed characteristics exceed the immediate, limited concerns of the author. The visions, however, plainly exploit several specific elements ignored in the interpretations. The lion's wings, for example, are plucked off, while the bear with the three ribs in its mouth is told to devour much flesh. Less plausible is the suggestion that the author deliberately develops extraneous elements in the visions as literary decorations, without a thought for their bearing on the interpretations. If such were the case, it is hard to imagine how irrelevant trivia of this sort should ever come to feature so prominently in both visions.

And I looked until *a big sword was given to the sheep*, and the sheep went out against all the wild animals to kill them, and all the animals and birds of heaven fled before them.[24]

Here it might be argued that the sheep, (the secondary subject), have become humanized in order to accommodate the requirements of the human story (the primary subject) which the author wishes to convey.[25] If, however, the author were to add, "The sheep with the big sword are my people Israel, *who shall scatter the enemy with their horns*," then it would be clear that the sheep image is meant to be taken seriously, since the secondary subject has now influenced the primary subject. In both of the following examples drawn from Daniel, (one from chapter 7 and the other from chapter 8), the secondary subject acts upon the primary subject.

(i) *Dan 7:7, 23*
After this I saw in the night visions, and behold, a fourth beast, terrible and dreadful and exceedingly strong; and it had great iron teeth; *it devoured and broke in pieces, and stamped the residue with its feet.*

Thus he said: As for the fourth beast, there shall be a fourth kingdom on earth, which shall be different from all the kingdoms, and *it shall devour the whole earth, and trample it down, and break it to pieces.*

This case of interaction indicates the author's interest in the fourth beast as an image: it successfully transforms or filters the reader's perception of the primary subject, so that the fourth kingdom appears more "beast-like" than it otherwise would.

(ii) *Dan 8:25*
By his cunning he shall make deceit prosper under his hand, and in his own mind he shall magnify himself. Without warning he shall destroy many; and he shall even rise up against the Prince of princes; but, by no human hand, *he shall be broken.*

This example is of particular interest. Here, in the interpretation of the vision, it is stated that Antiochus, the little horn of the vision, shall be "broken." Usage of *šbr* in this verse almost certainly harks back to its prior appearance in the vision (vss. 7, 8 cf. v. 22), where the horns of the ram and the great horn of the he-goat are likewise broken. That the verb should reappear in the literal context of the interpretation indicates that one of the *ad hoc* implications of the horn-image of the vision (the secondary subject) has acted upon the primary subject, Antiochus. His death is now described in appropriate "horn language." Interestingly, nowhere in the vision itself is

---

[24] Knibb 1978, 2:214

[25] Actually, the human element informing the animal symbolism of 1 Enoch 85–90 has a more complicated background. See our discussion in Chapter Four.

10

any such fate specifically ascribed to the little horn: all the reader learns is that the sanctuary attacked by the little horn is one day to be restored. This peculiarity underscores the semantic importance of the little horn as a visionary symbol: it actually *borrows* one of the connotations exhibited by the previous horns of the vision and transfers it to its own referent, the "king of bold countenance" of the interpretation (Antiochus) (vss. 23f.). This shift contradicts the popular belief that the little horn is a "blosse Wirklichkeitsschilderung,"[26] created by the author simply to make room in the vision for the career of Antiochus and his anticipated demise. If such were the sole intent of the author, it is incredible that he should have neglected to represent the subject dearest to his heart—the death of Antiochus—somewhere in the vision. Instead of Antiochus' anticipated death shaping the horn image, the process is clearly reversed: The Antiochus of history, declares the interpretation, is to be destroyed in the manner of a horn.

These two cases of interaction in Daniel 7 and 8 give rise to the following observations:

Firstly, it is to be expected that the most specific cases of interaction should occur in the interpretations of the fourth beast of chapter 7 and the little horn of chapter 8. In each chapter, the first beasts are passed over relatively briefly in the interpretation. In chapter 7, only one verse (v. 17) is given to explaining the first three beasts, whereas eight verses are required for the fourth beast (vss. 19–26). Similarly, the interpretation in chapter 8 devotes only three verses (vss. 20–22) to the ram, the he-goat and the four horns, but requires a further three verses (vss. 23–25) for the little horn alone. These examples of interaction, therefore, need not be taken as representing the only possible instances occurring in these chapters. If anything, they suggest how the exegete might set out to interpret the remaining symbols.[27]

Secondly, both cases of interaction serve to remind the exegete that the implicative complexes connected with the secondary subject are, in each instance, already prescribed in the vision, and are not to be sought independently in some open-ended system of connotations that may happen to commend itself to the reader's imagination. The fourth kingdom is the fourth beast, for example, not because this peculiar species commonly grazes on the foothills of that kingdom or happens to be a favourite pet of the emperor's daughter, but, in the first place, because the kingdom, like the

---

[26] Junker 1932, 67.

[27] This, of course, is only one possibility. See our discussion regarding the semantics of various metaphor clusters in Chapter Three.

beast,[28] "devours, tramples down, and breaks in pieces" its enemies. The fourth beast, therefore, is first and foremost a warrior beast, and the only additional connotations which the exegete may safely admit are those which demonstrably build upon this fact. Similarly, Antiochus is the little horn, not because he plays music on a horn, eats from a cornucopia or erects horns on his altar, but because he does the sorts of things that horns are seen to do in the vision. In this way, the invitation to explore the ancient world of art and literature for new connotations is sharply limited by implicit standards of relevance. Hundreds of associations with lions, bears, panthers, rams, he-goats and horns are simply and flatly declared irrelevant. To pursue them without constant regard to the *ad hoc* implicative complex already established by the author in each vision would be a mistaken extension of the metaphorical process.[29]

Conclusion

To sum up, our application of a tension or interaction view of metaphor to Daniel 7 and 8 shows the animal images of the visions to be semantically important for the following reasons: (1) The animal visions are more developed than the corresponding interpretations; and (2) both Daniel 7 and 8 exhibit clear cases of interaction, whereby the secondary subject acts upon the primary subject. In view of this, we shall proceed in the following chapters to examine the animal images in closer detail and in their broader linguistic and extralinguistic contexts.

---

[28] In saying this, we acknowledge the function of comparison or resemblance in the interaction process. See Ricoeur 1978, 173–215.
[29] Adapted from Booth 1978, 54.

PART II

"The king of Greece is a he-goat *with a horn between its eyes, four horns and a little horn . . ."*

CHAPTER 2

Visions of mantic monsters

Introduction

Although Daniel 7 and 8 mention animals such as the lion, bear, panther, ram and he-goat, it is a stubborn fact that not one of the beasts described in these chapters is entirely recognizable in the natural world. In chapter 7, both the lion and the panther are equipped with bird's wings, the bear is raised up on one side, and the panther has four heads, while the fourth beast has ten horns, an additional little horn with human eyes and a mouth, as well as clawed feet. In chapter 8, the ram has one horn higher than the other, while the he-goat carries a conspicuous horn between his eyes, which, when broken, is replaced by four large horns as well as an additional little horn.

Anomalous forms such as these present a striking contrast to the zoologically identifiable prophetic symbols of Amos 7:1–3 (locusts) and Hos 13:7–8 (lion, bear and panther).[1]

It is obvious that embellishments of this sort facilitate, in part, the historical concerns of the author. (Compare, for example, the ten horns of the fourth beast and the ten kings proceeding from the fourth kingdom; the four horns of the he-goat and the four divisions of the Macedonian empire). Such instances of correspondence, however, fail to account for those peculiarities of the animals which are seemingly irrelevant to the interpretations.[2] Just why a horned beast should have claws instead of hooves, for example, remains as much a mystery as ever.[3]

In this chapter, we shall argue that the peculiar physical characteristics ascribed to the various beasts are ultimately traceable to Mesopotamian mantic wisdom traditions.[4] Such a background is suggested by the context in which the visions appear in the book of Daniel. The author's sympathies are with the *mśkylym* or "wise" of chapters 11 and 12, within whose circles the visions of Daniel probably originated.[5] Daniel himself functions as a

---

[1] Cf. Koch 1983, 430–431.

[2] See Chapter One above.

[3] Similarly, certain details emerge in the interpretations which are not obviously represented in the visions, e.g., the $3\frac{1}{2}$ years (Dan 7:25) and the destruction of Antiochus (Dan 8:25). Cf. Porter 1905, 126.

[4] Müller (1972, 268–293) explores the relation of mantic wisdom to apocalyptic. Cf. also Collins 1975, 218–234; Bauckham 1978, 13–15.

[5] Collins 1975, 231.

wise courtier in Babylon, and it is in this capacity that he receives the visions of chapters 7 and 8.[6] Admittedly, important antecedents to apocalyptic dream-interpretation are also to be found in OT prophecy (e.g., Ezekiel 37; Zechariah 1–6).[7] Nevertheless, the fact that it is Daniel the Chaldean who interprets Nebuchadnezzar's dream in chapter 2 suggests a connection with mantic wisdom in the case of the visions of chapters 7 and 8, which also require an interpretation, albeit by an angel. Further intimations of such a connection are to be found in the so-called Akkadian Prophecies,[8] some of which show striking similarities to the book of Daniel.[9] Among these are the Marduk and Šulgi prophetic speeches[10] and the Dynastic Prophecy,[11] whose phraseology is indebted to Mesopotamian omen literature.[12] As Grayson has put it:

What could be more natural for the authors of these texts than to draw upon their extensive scribal education in omen literature (prognostic texts make up the single largest category in Ashurbanipal's library) for their "predictions"?[13]

The *Šumma izbu* series

Of the many divination series in ancient Mesopotamia, one of the most important was the series *Šumma izbu* ("If an anomaly ..."), a collection of at least twenty-four tablets in which anomalous human and animal births and their bearing on the future affairs of both individuals and state are delineated.[14] In the unpublished catalogue K. 13280, it is ranked second only to the astrological omens.[15] Four copies of the series were found in Ashurbanipal's library.[16] Exemplars of the series represent a wide geographical distribution, having been found at many sites both inside and outside of Mesopotamia. They are written in Akkadian, Hittite, Hurrian and

---

[6] Cf. Collins 1975, 232.

[7] Müller 1972, 285–286.

[8] Surveyed in Ringgren 1983, 379–386.

[9] Zimmern 1903, 392; Grayson and Lambert 1964, 10; Hallo 1966, 240–242; Grayson 1975, 20–22; Lambert 1978.

[10] Borger 1971, 3–21.

[11] Grayson 1975, 24–37.

[12] Grayson 1975, 15–16.

[13] Grayson 1975, 16.

[14] Leichty 1970.

[15] Leichty 1970, 7.

[16] Leichty 1970, 21. On p. 26, Leichty notes: "It must be stressed that, as in the case of the addition of omens, the ordering and standardization of the text into the twenty-four tablet Kuyunjik edition was probably not the work of a single man at a fixed point of time, but was rather a continuing process covering a long period of time in several different places. It must also be remembered, because of this, that when the text was standardized it did not result in a single edition, but rather in several parallel editions each with varying details, dependent on their source."

Ugaritic, and are to be dated from the Old Babylonian period (ca. 1600 BCE) to the Seleucid period (ca. 100 BCE),[17] during which at least one copy of the series was made at the last scribal school of Babylonia, in Uruk.[18] Although most of the omens discussed probably occurred in nature, others are mentioned which were clearly impossible, obviously in an attempt to make the series all-inclusive.[19]

Daniel 7 and 8 and *Šumma izbu*

Since both the Daniel visions and the *Šumma izbu* series offer an interpretation of animal anomalies in relation to future political conflicts, closer comparison of the two works commends itself. The following parallels, we believe, indicate that the animal anomalies of Daniel 7 and 8 bear the mark of mantic wisdom. All citations from *Šumma izbu* are according to Leichty:

Daniel	*Šumma izbu*
7:5 And behold, another beast, a second one, like a bear. *It was raised up on one side* ...	XIV 10 If an anomaly's *right shoulder is raised*—your enemy will carry off the power of your country; a palace official will die; birth of a moron in your land. XIV 11 If an anomaly's *left shoulder is raised*—the prince will carry off the power of the enemy land; birth of a moron in the enemy land.
7:5 it had three *ribs in its mouth* between its teeth ...	XVII 16' If an anomaly holds *its lung(s) in its mouth*—a strong king [...]
7:6 After this I looked, and lo, another, like a leopard ... and *the beast had four heads*; and dominion was given to it.	VII A 1–2 If an anomaly has *two heads*, but (only) one neck—the king will conquer wherever he turns; he will conquer a land which does not belong to him (var.), the king will have no opponent.
7:7 After this I saw in the night visions, and behold, a fourth beast, ... and *it had ten horns*.	Several multiple-horned anomalies are described in Tablet IX, e.g., IX 64': "If an anomaly has *one horn on its left and two on its*

---

[17] Leichty 1970, 20.
[18] Leichty 1970, 21.
[19] Leichty 1970, 20.

17

7:8 ... and behold, *in this horn were eyes* ...

forehead, and none on the right— overthrow of the army of the prince; the army of the enemy [...]"

X 42' *If an anomaly's eyes are on the top of its head*—end of the reign. (Cf. also X 63': "If an anomaly's eyes are normal, but it has *a third one on its hoof*— an enemy will overthrow the prince's auxiliary troops").

7:19 the fourth beast ... with its ... *claws* of bronze ...

XIX 15' If a cow gives birth and (the calf's) *fore-feet are like the paws of a lion*—the prince's weapon [...]
XIV 47 If an anomaly's *four legs are like the paws of a lion*—[...]

8:3 ... a ram standing on the bank of the river. It had two horns; and both horns were high, but *one was higher than the other*, and the higher one came up last.

IX 56' If an anomaly's *right horn is long and its left one short*—the land of the enemy ...
IX 57' If an anomaly's *left horn is long and its right one short* —the land of the prince ...

8:5 ... and the goat had *a conspic- uous horn between his eyes*.

IX 32' If an anomaly has *only one horn, and it protrudes from its head*—weapon of Sargon; the land of the prince will expand; the weapons will be strong and the king will have no opponent.
IX 33' If an anomaly has *only one horn, and it protrudes from the top (of its head)*—the land of the prince will expand; [...] your enemy will reside in the land; the king will have auxil- iary troops and will overthrow the land of his enemy.
IX 34' If an anomaly has *only one horn, and it protrudes from its forehead*—weapon of Sargon.

8:8 ... the great horn was broken, and instead of it there came up *four* conspicuous *horns* toward the *four winds of heaven*.

V 29 If a ewe gives birth to a lion, and it has *four horns* on the right and left—the prince will rule the (*four*) *quarters*.

As the above comparison shows, nearly all of the peculiar features characterizing the animals of the Daniel visions are anticipated in the *Šumma izbu* series. Common to both works are references to animals raised

18

on one side, multiple-headed animals,[20] animals with multiple horns, animals with displaced eyes, horned animals with claws, animals with horns of unequal length, and unicorns. Although animals with wings (cf. the lion and panther) and little horns (cf. the fourth beast and the he-goat) find no clear mention in *Šumma izbu*,[21] the above comparisons raise the likelihood that phenomena such as these were regarded, in the first place, as actual or hypothetical sports of nature.[22]

Historical omens

Twenty-nine historical omens are recorded in the main text of *Šumma izbu*.[23] A further seven occur in the Old Babylonian tablet YOS 10 56, which is a forerunner to Tablets V–XVII of the standardized version.[24] The specificity of these apodoses brings us one step closer to the historical interpreta-

---

[20] For reference to anomalies with up to 4 heads, see the untranslated text g (VAT 17293) which almost certainly belongs to Tablet VIII of *Šumma izbu* (Leichty 1970, 113).

[21] However, cf. bird-like anomalies in XVII 53'; XVIII 28'; XX 25'.

[22] Cf. Jastrow (1914, 60–61, 63), who argues that winged monsters in Mesopotamian art reflect birth-omen notions. "Another little horn" (cf. Dan 7:8; 8:9) is mentioned in Robert Plot's report of malformed sheep observed in seventeenth-century Oxfordshire. Also included in the account of this British natural historian are references to multiple-horned sheep, a unicorn, as well as sheep with horns "bending round to the cheeks"—all of which find specific mention in *Šumma izbu*: "But there are much stranger sheep, though perhaps not so profitable, at Ricot in the Park of the Right Honorable the Lord Norreys, brought hither from some other parts of England or Wales, but now breeding here: Of which, some of them at first had *six or eight horns apiece*, but the number upon mixture of their generation with other sheep is since diminsh'd. However, there remain still two of them with very strange heads, *having each four horns*; one of them with two larger ones issuing from the top of its head, bending forward, and two side ones coming out from under its ears, and bending round towards its mouth, as in Tab. 10. Fig. 10. And the other having two large horns standing pretty upright on its head, and two side ones proceeding from under the ears like the former, and *bending round to the cheeks*, into which they would grow (and so in the whole kind) were they not prevented by being timely cut off, as in Tab. 10. Fig. 11. And as these are remarkable for their many horns, there was another sheep once there, that excelled all the rest, in its being a *Unicorn*, having a single horn growing almost in the middle of its fore-head, 21 inches long, with annulary protuberances round it, and a little twisted about the middle, as in Tab. 10. Fig. 12. There was, 'tis true, *another little horn* grew on the same head, but so inconsiderable, that it was hid under the wool. This head is still preserved by the Honorable the Lord Norreys, and is now to be seen nailed up at Ricot on the North side of the Hall" (italics ours) (Plot 1677, 188–189). Prof. Koch kindly draws my attention to the following report in *Die Welt* (Jan 6, 1983, p. 18): "Jede Menge Hörner—AP, Berlin. Eine Ueberraschung erlebte ein Viehzüchter im Norden Bulgariens, als ein Mutterschaf bei einem einzigen Wurf gleich drei Lämmer zur Welt brachte. Nach der Ostberliner Nachrichtenagentur ADN hatte ihm die Natur noch ein weiteres Schnippchen geschlagen: Die drei Böckchen haben zusammen elf Hörner. Eins hat gar keinen 'Kopfschmuck' und die beiden anderen zierten fünf beziehungsweise sechs Hörner."

[23] Leichty 1970, 26. For a discussion of the Old Babylonian "historical" omens, see Goetze 1947, 253–265; Finkelstein 1963, 462–472; Reiner 1974, 257–261.

[24] Leichty 1970, 26, 23.

tion accompanying the vision of Daniel 8, in which beasts or horns are identified with specific kings:

Dan 8:20–21
As for the ram which you saw with the two horns, these are *the kings of Media and Persia.* And the he-goat is the *king of Greece*; and the great horn between his eyes is *the first king.*

Šumma izbu
IX 34' If an anomaly has only one horn, and it protrudes from its forehead—weapon of *Sargon.*

XII 28 If an anomaly has whiskers— the land [...] will bring tribute; ditto (i.e. same protasis)—*the king of Ammuru* [sic] will seize the throne; [...]

V 97 If a ewe gives birth to a tiger—attack of *Elam.*

YOS 10 56 42 If an anomaly is like a fox—reign of Enlil; the land will prosper; *the king of Sumer* will rule the land.

XVI A If an anomaly's stomach is in the area of its right lung— *the king of Amurru* will kill *the king of Akkad.*

Less specific apodoses offer a further point of comparison with Daniel:

Dan 8:23
... *a king of bold countenance,* one who understands riddles, shall arise.

Šumma izbu IX 44'
If an anomaly's horns protrude from its forehead—omen of *a despotic king*; the prince will take the land of his enemy.

Dan 7:24
As for the ten horns, *out of this kingdom ten kings shall arise, and another shall arise after them*; he shall be different from the former ones, and shall put down three kings.

Šumma izbu VII 80'
If an anomaly has two heads, two spines, six (sets of) ribs, two tails, six feet, three eyes, (and) three bases—*the sons of the king will fight among themselves, and one among them will fall.*

Finally, both in Daniel and in *Šumma izbu*, an animal anomaly becomes the basis for a time prediction:

Dan 7:24–25
As for the ten horns ... another shall arise after them ... the saints of the Most High ...

Šumma izbu XX 19'
If a mare bears twins and they have one chest, two heads [...] two hips [...] normal feet,

20

shall be given into his hand
for *a time, two times, and
half a time*.

tail and hair—the days of the
prince will be long; [...] the
king will become strong; the
land will not be happy for *six
years*; its (the mare's) owner
will die.

Animal comparisons

In Daniel 7, the first three beasts are likened to, rather than identified with, a
lion, bear and panther respectively (vss. 4, 5, 6). Similarly, v. 13 describes
the cloud-riding figure as "one *like* a son of man."

As will shortly be shown below, this peculiarity is also paralleled in
numerous *Šumma izbu* texts. Apart from the omens derived from human
births (Tablets I–IV), the anomalies recorded in Tablets V, XVIII–XXIV are
all born to domestic animals (sheep, goats, cattle, horses, pigs, dogs,
gazelles). Although the term *izbu* ("anomaly") occurring in Tablets
VI–XVII may refer to any malformed newborn animal, it usually refers to
sheep. This is evident from the fact that many of the Old Babylonian omens
(beginning "if an *izbu*") were transferred to Tablet V (beginning "if a ewe")
of the main series:[25]

YOS 10 56

3 If an anomaly is like a
wolf—there will be plague in
the land.

40 If an anomaly is like a lion—
omen of Narām-Sin who ruled
the world.

42 If an anomaly is like a
fox—reign of Enlil; the land
will prosper; the king of
Sumer will rule the land.

51 If an anomaly is (like) a tiger—
there will be a despotic king in the
land.

Šumma izbu V

90 If a ewe gives birth to a
wolf—there will be plague in
the land; madness; destruction
of the land; disease of the
herds.

1 If a ewe gives birth to a lion—
the weapons (which were) abandoned
will be raised; the king will
have no opponent.

94 If a ewe gives birth to a
fox—reign of Enlil; he will
cause the years of Sargon to be
in the land; that ox-fold will
increase; ditto (i.e. same protasis)—the king will reign
peacefully into his old age.

97 If a ewe gives birth to a
tiger—attack of Elam.

---

[25] Leichty 1970, 3 cf. n. 4.

21

The above comparisons also reveal that the "wolf," "lion," "fox" and "tiger," which are born to a ewe in Tablet V, are, in fact, sheep whose appearance is merely suggestive of these various predators. This is proved by the corresponding Old Babylonian omens which use *kīma* ("like") in the protasis.[26] Such being the case, the three "predators" and the "son of man" in Daniel 7 may, in fact, be domestic animals comparable to birth anomalies already recorded in *Šumma izbu*:

Daniel 7	*Šumma izbu*
v. 4 The first was like a lion and had eagles' wings ...	V 50 If a ewe gives birth to a lion, and it has the head of a *ḫūqu*-bird—the son of a widow will seize the throne.
v. 5 And behold, another beast, a second one, like a bear ...	V 107 If a ewe gives birth to a bear—a person with no right to the throne will seize it.
v. 6 After this I looked, and lo, another, like a leopard ...	V 96 If a ewe gives birth to a leopard—a prince will seize universal kingship.
v. 13 I saw in the night visions, and behold, with the clouds of heaven there came one like a son of man ...	V 51 If a ewe gives birth to a lion, and it has a human face— ...
	XVIII 33' If a goat gives birth to a human, (var.), a cripple—[...]
	XX 24' If a mare gives birth to a human—the whole land will have good fortune.

Šumma izbu and related apocalyptic texts

Various anomalies classified in *Šumma izbu* also reappear in connection with the following works, which, like Daniel 7 and 8, may be described as apocalyptic: the Bokkhoris Lamb tradition, 1 Enoch 85–90, Testament of Joseph 19, and the Revelation of John.

The Bokkhoris Lamb tradition

Generally considered comparable to Jewish apocalyptic[27] is the Hellenistic-Egyptian tradition of the prophetic lamb which appeared in the reign of King Bokkhoris (718–712 BCE).[28] This lamb purportedly delivered a series

---

[26] Cf. also the horns and wool of various "lions" born to a ewe in V 15–29, 77.

[27] Cf. McCown 1925, 357f.; Koch 1972, 34–35; Griffiths 1983, 285–287.

[28] See Krall 1898, 3–11; Janssen 1954, 17–29; Kákosy 1966, 344–345; Dunand 1977, 50–51.

of predictions concerning events occurring in Egypt during the following nine hundred years. After a long period marked by social upheaval and injustice, Egypt would finally enter an era of political stability. Since Hellenistic oracle literature is largely based on eastern prototypes,[29] the tradition invites comparison with *Šumma izbu*. Aelian (b. ca. 170 CE) describes the lamb in considerable detail, in a passage which should probably be traced to Manetho (3rd. century BCE).[30] His description suggests a Siamese-twin anomaly comparable to the numerous varieties mentioned in Tablet VIII of *Šumma izbu*:

Aelian, De natura animalium

XII 3 The Egyptians assert (though they are far from convincing me), they assert, I say, that in the days of the far-famed Bocchoris *a Lamb was born with eight feet and two tails*, and that it spoke. They say also that *this Lamb had two heads and four horns* ...[31]

Šumma izbu

VIII 84' If an anomaly has *two heads*, four shoulders, *two tails*, (and) *eight feet*—one throne will overthrow the other.

1 Enoch 85–90

The Enoch tradition, like that of Daniel, is rooted in the Jewish encounter with Babylonian culture.[32] Although an encyclopedic interest in cosmological wisdom characterizes 1 Enoch, the same work also indicates a certain awareness of mantic wisdom in 7:1 and 8:3.[33] Several parallels with *Šumma izbu* occur in the Maccabean[34] chapters 85–90, a passage whose animal imagery in many ways resembles that of Daniel 7 and 8 (see Chapter Four below):[35]

a. 1 En 90:9–10 utilizes the unicorn motif, which, as already noted, occurs in both Daniel and *Šumma izbu*:

1 En 90:9–10

And I looked

Dan 8:5

the goat had *a*

Šumma izbu IX 32'

If an anomaly has *only*

[29] Koch 1972, 35.

[30] Krall 1898, 5; Koch 1966a, 91. However, according to Meyer (1909, 135–136), Apion (1st. century CE) added to Manetho's earlier account the peculiar features of the lamb reported in Aelian.

[31] Scholfield 1959, 11.

[32] Cf. Milik 1976, 14–18, 29–31, 33, 37f., 277.

[33] Bauckham 1978, 16 n. 40.

[34] For the Maccabean dating of these chapters, see Chapter Four below.

[35] All citations from 1 Enoch are according to Knibb 1978.

| until *a big horn grew on one of those sheep ...* and the rams saw it, and they all ran to it. | *conspicuous horn between his eyes.* | *one horn, and it pro- trudes from its head ...* |

b. Common to *Šumma izbu*, Daniel (see above), and 1 Enoch, is mention of various kinds of beasts or birds born to domestic animals:

1 Enoch

86:4 And I looked at them and saw, and behold, all of them let out their private parts like horses and began to mount the cows of the bulls, and they all became pregnant and bore elephants and camels and asses.

89:10 And they [the bulls] began to beget wild-animals and birds, so that there arose from them every kind of species: *lions, tigers, wolves, dogs,* hyenas, wild-boars, *foxes,* *badgers, pigs,* falcons, vultures, kites, eagles and *ravens*.

Šumma izbu

XVIII 16' If a goat gives birth to a *lion*—the king will exercise world rule; the army of the man will have no opponent.
V 97 If a ewe gives birth to a *tiger*—attack of Elam.
XVIII 17' If a goat gives birth to a *wolf*—the god [...]
XVIII 18' If a goat gives birth to a *dog*—the progeny of the herd will not prosper.
XVIII 24' If a goat gives birth to a *fox*—[...]
V 91 If a ewe gives birth to a *badger*—the land of the prince will prosper; the king will behave badly toward his land.
XX 22' If a mare gives birth to a *pig*, (var.), fox—the prince will die.
XX 25' If a mare gives birth to a *bird*—the whole land will enjoy abundant food.
XVIII 28' If a goat gives birth to a *raven*—[...]

c. Animal cannibalism is mentioned in both 1 Enoch and *Šumma izbu*:

1 En 87:1

... they [the bulls] began to gore one another and to *devour one anoter* ...

Šumma izbu XXIII 31'

If one dog *eats another* dog— that city will experience hard times.

24

d. The following parallel must remain tentative due to a break in the *Šumma izbu* text:

1 En 85:3

behold, a bull came out of
the earth, and that bull was
white; and after it a heifer
came out and with the *heifer*
came two bullocks, and *one of
them was black, and the other
red*.

Šumma izbu XIX 5'

If a *cow* gives birth and *red*
and *black* [. . .]

Testament of Joseph 19

To date, no consensus exists concerning either the original language, date or provenance of the Testaments. Proposed datings for the Testaments in their present form range from pre-Maccabean times (2nd. century BCE)[36] to ca. 150 CE.[37] Testament of Joseph 19 is a vision report with formal similarities to Daniel 7 and 8 and later apocalyptic works,[38] while its imagery and phraseology resemble certain sections of 1 Enoch 85–90.[39] Vss. 3–7, which occur only in the Armenian version, are probably part of the original text.[40] Two passages in Testament of Joseph 19 recall the imagery of *Šumma izbu*:

a. In a passage reminiscent of both Dan 7:8 and *Šumma izbu*, Test Jos 19:6 employs the motif of an additional horn:

Test Jos 19:6

And the horns of
the fourth bull were
elevated up to the
heavens and became a
wall for the flocks
and *another horn
flowered between the
horns*.[41]

Dan 7:8

I considered the
horns, and behold,
*there came up among
them another horn*,
a little one . . .

Šumma izbu IX 69'–70'

In an anomaly has *two
horns and a third one*
on the top (of its
head)—a land which
does not belong to
the prince will gather
to him [. . .]
If an anomaly has *two
horns and a third one*
on its forehead—the
prince will become
overpowering; [. . .]
the weapon [. . .]

---

[36] Becker 1970, 375.
[37] de Jonge 1971, 77–96; de Jonge 1975, 183–192.
[38] Koch 1966a, 88–89.
[39] Hultgård 1977, 214–215.
[40] Hultgård 1980, 96.
[41] Stone 1975, 55.

b. Mention of a sheep born to a woman occurs in both Test Jos 19:8 and *Šumma izbu*, but is absent from Daniel:

Test Jos 19:8 (Greek)	*Test Jos 19:8 (Armenian)*	*Šumma izbu I 14*
And I saw that a maiden, a virgin, was born from Judah, wearing a linen garment, and *from her went forth a lamb* without blemish and on its left hand there was, as it were, a lion, and all the beasts rushed against him and the lamb defeated them and destroyed them, trodding [sic] them under foot. [42]	And I saw in the middle of the horns a maiden, wearing a many-coloured garment, and *from her went forth a lamb* and on his right all the beasts and all the reptiles rushed forth and the lamb defeated them and destroyed them. [43]	*If a woman gives birth to a ram —* the prince will have no opponent.

Jeremias and others have sought to dismiss Test Jos 19:8 as a purely Christian interpolation. [44] The above comparison, however, suggests that the motif of a lamb born to a woman ultimately stems from mantic rather than Christian circles.

The Revelation of John

This late first-century Christian document alludes in 13:1–2 to the beasts of Daniel 7, and in 5:6 mentions a multiple-horned warrior lamb comparable to the multiple-horned he-goat of Daniel 8. Calls for "wisdom" in connection with the correct interpretation of John's animal anomalies in 13:18 and 17:9 indicate that John understands Christians to be the *mśkylym* referred to in Daniel 11 and 12. [45] The interpreting angel mentioned in 17:1, 7 is reminiscent of the heavenly interpreter of Dan 7:16 and 8:16, and, ultimately, of Daniel the wise courtier who himself interprets dreams and riddles in Babylon (Dan 2:25f.; 4:8f.; 5:11f.). We suggest the following comparisons with *Šumma izbu*:

a. Animals with multiple eyes:

---

[42] Hultgård 1980, 97.
[43] Hultgård 1980, 97.
[44] J. Jeremias 1966, 216–219.
[45] Beale 1980, 163–170.

Rev 5:6

I saw a Lamb ... with *seven*
eyes ...

Šumma izbu X 72'

If an anomaly has *six eyes*, (and)
they are normal, but three eyes are
on its forehead—attack of a usurper;
ditto (i.e. same protasis)—the
weapons which were not brought
there will attack the
prince.

b. Lion/lamb with multiple horns:

Rev 5:5–6

... lo, the *Lion* of the tribe
of Judah ... has conquered ...
And ... I saw a *Lamb* standing,
as though it had been slain,
with seven horns.

Šumma izbu V 29

If a *ewe* gives birth to a *lion*,
and it has *four horns* on the
right and left—the prince will
rule the four quarters.

c. Composite animals:

Rev 13:2

And the beast that I saw was
like a leopard, its feet were
like a bear's, and its mouth
was like a lion's mouth.

Šumma izbu XXI 11

If the anomaly of a mare has
feet like a lion, a head like
a dog, a tail like a pig, (and)
no hair—downfall of the prince;
the same omen—the king will
fall violently (cf. also YOS
56 48).

The significance of the *Šumma izbu* texts

Our comparison of the *Šumma izbu* texts with Daniel 7 and 8 and other
apocalyptic works gives rise to the following observations:

(1) It is clear that the animal anomalies in Daniel 7 and 8 cannot be
adequately treated in isolation, but belong to a wider context informing
Hellenistic, Jewish and Christian works alike over a period in excess of
three centuries.

(2) The fact that animal anomalies should characterize apocalyptic rather
than prophetic literature in Israel is to be explained in the light of that
nation's relatively late encounter with Mesopotamian mantic wisdom traditions.

(3) The ambiguity of the referents corresponding to the four beasts of
Daniel 7 (7:17), the horns of the fourth beast (7:24) and the little horn of the
he-goat (8:23) does not necessarily indicate the author's intention that his
visions be continually reapplied to new historical circumstances. To the
contrary, the author of Daniel believed that he himself was living in the time

27

of the end, and any thought of a reuse of his visions by later apocalyptic circles (e.g., as in 4 Ezra 11–12 and Revelation 13) would have been inconceivable. Rather, the multireferential nature of such images originates in the *Šumma izbu* tablets themselves, whose non-historical apodoses provided stock interpretations of anomalous births considered capable of occurring on any number of occasions.

(4) The unevenness characterizing the visions and the interpretations in Daniel 7 and 8—i.e., the fact that certain details in the visions find no specific correspondence in the interpretations and vice versa—[46]is comparable to a similar lack of detailed correspondence between protasis and apodosis in numerous birth-omen texts.

(5) Since the animal anomalies of *Šumma izbu* are limited to those born to sheep, goats, cattle, horses, dogs, pigs and gazelles, it is to be expected that in Daniel 7 and 8, the predators rather than the horned beasts should be described as comparisons. The "lion," "bear" and "panther" are only such in appearance, while the anomalous features of the remaining beasts are limited to their horns or hooves. (The fact that the ten-horned beast is neither named nor likened to any specific species is comparable to numerous birth-omen texts beginning "If an *izbu* ...").

(6) Hooker, who notes that the comparative form in Daniel 7 is used not only of the predators, but also of the son of man, rightly argues that the latter figure is not necessarily a member of the human species.[47] Since our parallels with *Šumma izbu* extend across both chapters 7 and 8 of Daniel, it should also be said that the reference to "one like a son of man" in 7:13 occurs in the context of two visions replete with descriptions of animal anomalies. If our argument holds that the comparative form describing the predators stems from birth-omen traditions, then it is probable that the comparative particle in 7:13 should be interpreted against a similar background. In this regard, it is perhaps significant that the enthronement of the son of man in Daniel 7 is in several points comparable to the enthronement of an anomalous lamb with seven horns and seven eyes in Revelation 5,[48] who, later in the work, is depicted as the opposite number of a ten-horned *Mischwesen* with characteristics drawn from all four beasts of Daniel 7 (Rev 13:1–8; 17:14 etc.).

(7) Since the *Šumma izbu* series was consulted throughout the history of its existence,[49] we may conclude that, as late as ca. 100 BCE, the animals it describes were still regarded in Mesopotamia as literal possibilities, even

---

[46] Cf. n. 3 above.
[47] Hooker 1967, 11–13.
[48] Cf. Collins 1976, 213–215.
[49] Leichty 1970, 7.

though the more fantastic forms obviously had never occurred in nature. The anomalies of Daniel 7 and 8, therefore, were presumably within the range of biological possibility, as defined by significant numbers of the author's Mesopotamian contemporaries. In a Mesopotamian context, such beasts were neither ridiculous nor impossible, but ominous. Probably the author himself shared such a view, since both chapters are included in a book betraying a demonstrable interest in Chaldean wisdom, as noted at the beginning of this chapter. If such were the case, the animal anomalies in these visions originally had an evocative power by virtue of their stylistic dependence on Mesopotamian omen literature, rather than because of any perceived literal absurdity.

Conclusion

We began this chapter with the observation that not one of the beasts in the visions of Daniel 7 and 8 is entirely recognizable in the zoological world. Since many of the physical peculiarities of these animals are seemingly irrelevant to the interpretations, we proposed to account for the animal anomalies by considering them in the light of Mesopotamian mantic wisdom. Numerous parallels were then drawn between various anomalies described in the *Šumma izbu* series and those appearing in both the Daniel visions and several comparable apocalyptic works ranging from the 3rd. century BCE to the 1st. century CE. On the basis of these comparisons, we concluded that the evocative power of the animal anomalies in Daniel 7 and 8 does not stem from any perceived literal absurdity, but from their stylistic associations with Mesopotamian omen traditions.

PART III

"The king of Greece is a he-goat with a horn between its eyes, four horns, and a little horn *which attacks the stars, the truth and the sanctuary*"

CHAPTER 3
Metaphor clusters

Introduction

In Part II, we discussed the *physical* peculiarities of the animals of Daniel 7 and 8. In Part III, we now focus on the *functional* characteristics of these animals. Here we shall seek answers to the following sorts of questions: Why should beasts emerge from the sea (Daniel 7)? Why should they come into judgment (Daniel 7)? Why should the horn of a he-goat attack the host, the truth and the temple (Daniel 8)? Why should beasts with characteristics such as these also function as political symbols (Daniel 7 and 8)?

Traditionally, only the first of these questions has aroused serious exegetical interest, since references in the visions to the judgment, the host, the truth and the temple are generally regarded as historical allusions to the Seleucid crisis and its expected outcome, which at best recall traditions bearing no obvious relation to the animal images of Daniel 7 and 8.[1]

It is methodologically unsound, however, to assume from the beginning that historical concerns necessarily led the author of the visions to mix his metaphors. The mere inclusion of historical elements in the context of the symbolic visions requires that the exegete recognize in such elements a "concomitant" meaning—be it ever so slight—in which both literal and symbolic meanings are simultaneously present.[2] A temple that is vulnerable to horned attack, for example, is not the exact equivalent of the literal temple in Jerusalem, although the latter may be simultaneously in view. Such being the case, the exegete should first of all carefully consider the extent to which these historico-symbolic images might be said to be "at home" within the context of the animal symbols. Might such images, along with the animal symbols, belong to a "metaphor cluster"—viz., a group of metaphors already linked by some common idea? Such is already suggested both by the logical development of the vision of chapter 7, and by the close semantic relationship evident between the he-goat- and little horn visions of chapter 8. (In the former instance, the judgment of the beasts is precipitated

---

[1] For example, Collins (1977, 101) compares the Ancient of Days of Daniel 7 with the Ugaritic El, who in *Ugaritica 5*, Text 2 is said to judge. The same author traces the imagery of the stars in Daniel 8 back to Isa 14:12–15 (p. 106f.), while the temple is viewed as a symbol for the kingdom (p. 165).
[2] Cf. Barfield 1960, 48.

by the blasphemies of the little horn of the fourth beast (7:8–12). Beasts and judgment, consequently, are to some extent logically interrelated. In chapter 8, the he-goat- and little horn visions are semantically linked by the verbs *šlk* and *rms*. In verse 7, these verbs describe the literal action of the he-goat against the ram: he "cast him down (*šlk*) to the ground and trampled upon (*rms*) him." In verses 10, 11, 12 and 13, the expression is repeatedly extended to describe the action of the little horn against the host or stars, the sanctuary and the truth: all are either "cast down" (*šlk, npl*) or "trampled upon" (*rms*) in a manner clearly reminiscent of the he-goat vision).[3] Secondly, since both Daniel 7 and 8 share a common interest in beasts and horns as political symbols, it will be necessary to consider whether a single metaphor cluster might account for the beasts of both chapters considered as a unit, as well as their suitability as political symbols.

In this chapter, we shall review a representative selection of metaphor clusters proposed by exegetes of Daniel 7 and 8. We shall briefly note the limitations of each hypothesis, and then propose an interpretative model for a metaphor cluster which accounts for the animals of both chapters as well as their functional characteristics, including their symbolic function. In the remaining chapters of this section, we shall submit both synchronic and diachronic evidence for a metaphor cluster in Daniel 7 and 8 which not only corresponds to our interpretative model, but also takes into consideration the physical peculiarities of the animals discussed in Part II.

Metaphor clusters in Daniel 7 and 8—previous proposals

To date, exegetes have failed to reach a consensus concerning either the identification or the interpretation of metaphor clusters in Daniel 7 and 8. The following proposals are representative:

a. *Daniel 7*. Gunkel sought to find traces of the four beasts of Daniel 7 in the Babylonian creation epic, *Enuma eliš*.[4] Many scholars have followed his lead.[5] Others have compared the beasts with Yamm/Lotan of Canaanite mythology.[6] Another view explains the first three animals as Babylonian

---

[3] Cf. Beekman 1974, 134: "If, in a particular context, there are non-figurative items which stand in a close semantic relationship to the metaphorical image(s) being used, then this also indicates that the figure is a live one. The speaker or writer deliberately calls to the listener's or reader's mind images chosen from that setting. For example, in Mark 1:17, Jesus says, 'I will make you to become fishers of men.' The immediate context refers to the Sea of Galilee, fishermen, nets, a ship, and hired servants. The whole setting is appropriate to fishing and so we conclude that this metaphor is a live one."

[4] Gunkel 1895, 331–335.

[5] See Koch 1980, 95.

[6] In particular Collins 1977, 96–104.

astrological symbols.[7] Yet another group of exegetes have likened the beasts to Mesopotamian art forms.[8] According to Porteous, the beasts have a heraldic character.[9] Junker described the first three animals as the most dangerous predators known to Israel,[10] while Sahlin has suggested a parallel between the four beasts and the four living creatures of Ezekiel 1.[11] Wittstruck explains the lion, bear and panther against a background of treaty curses dealing with devouring animals.[12] Finally, several scholars see an intended contrast between the beasts representing the hostile nations and the man-like figure whose kingdom replaces theirs at the end-time.[13] Farrer traces this contrast to the priestly account of creation in Genesis,[14] while others have suggested Psalm 8, Psalm 80, and Eze 34:31 as possible sources for this idea.[15]

b. *Daniel 8*. Several exegetes of Daniel 8 have followed Burkitt and Cumont, who identified the ram and he-goat as Babylonian astrological symbols.[16] An earlier view which treats these animal motifs as traditional OT metaphors for rulers and warriors (cf. Eze 34:17; 39:18)[17] is still represented.[18] According to Collins, the heart of Daniel 8 lies in the vision of the little horn (vss. 8–12), which is modelled on the myth of Helal ben Shachar (Isa 14:12–15).[19] Finally, Ford seeks to interpret the animal symbolism of both Daniel 7 and 8 in the light of Jewish dietary laws.[20]

The hypotheses we have reviewed are subject to the following limitations:

Firstly, most clusters proposed for Daniel 7 account for only some of the specific animals there described. Of the various beasts accompanying Tiamat in *Enuma eliš*, only the lion is mentioned in Daniel 7. In the Canaanite combat myths, no specific parallels can be found for any of the beasts of Daniel 7. Advocates of the astrological hypothesis have produced no astral symbol comparable to the fourth beast. Attempts to explain the four beasts as Mesopotamian iconographic motifs are hindered by the fact that the bear and panther are rarely represented, while the winged lion (as opposed to

[7] Caquot 1955, 5–13; 1967, 37–71; Delcor 1968, 290–312; 1971, 144–147.
[8] Kraeling 1933, 228; Herzfeld 1947, 831–832; Noth 1966, 210; Koch 1966b, 55.
[9] Porteous 1979, 105.
[10] Junker 1932, 37.
[11] Sahlin 1969, 48.
[12] Wittstruck 1978, 100–102.
[13] E.g., Koch 1961, 24; Casey 1979, 19, 25–27.
[14] Farrer 1951, 258–262.
[15] Hooker 1967, 18–19.
[16] Cumont 1909, 273; Bentzen 1952, 69; Hengel 1974, 1:184; Collins 1977, 107; Porteous 1979, 122.
[17] Cf. von Lengerke 1835, 367, 369.
[18] Lacocque 1979, 160.
[19] Collins 1977, 106.
[20] Ford 1979, 203–212.

numerous winged *Mischwesen*) is relatively uncommon in the ancient world.[21] Porteous' proposal that the animals are heraldic images rests solely on the first beast's identification with Nebuchadnezzar in Jer 50:44 (cf. Eze 17:3). Junker, who finds OT antecedents for the lion, bear and panther of Daniel 7, is forced to conclude that the fourth beast is a product of the author's own fancy. Sahlin's attempt to compare Daniel 7 with Ezekiel 1 is inadequate because the identity of the four beasts in Ezekiel differs considerably from that of the four beasts of Daniel 7. Wittstruck's treaty-curse hypothesis has questionable textual support,[22] and, at best, still fails to account for the fourth beast of Daniel 7. OT parallels to Daniel 7's man-beast contrast are presently inconclusive, and require further development: the lion, bear, panther and ten-horned beast of Daniel 7 have not been shown to bear any noticeable relation to the birds, animals and fish of Gen 1:28, the sheep, oxen, beasts, birds and fish of Ps 8:8–9, the boar of Ps 80:14 or the wild beasts of Eze 34:25.

Secondly, none of the metaphor clusters proposed for either Daniel 7 or 8 successfully accounts for the physical and functional peculiarities (in Black's terms, the *ad hoc* implicative complex) ascribed to the animals in each of the visions. Astral-geographic symbols, for example, are yet to be shown to resemble the physical anomalies recorded in Daniel 7 and 8.[23] Such symbols, furthermore, neither emerge from the sea, come into judgment (cf. chapter 7), fight on riverbanks nor attack temples (cf. chapter 8). Moreover, by thus ignoring the *ad hoc* implicative complexes, advocates of the above hypotheses are logically obliged to distinguish between the supposed origins of the animal images and the actual use made of them by the

---

[21] Cf. Staub 1978, 354–355.

[22] Rimbach 1978, 565–566.

[23] However, a winged lion representing Akkad is to be found on VAT 7847 from Seleucid Uruk (see Weidner 1967, 19 and Tafel 6). Birth-omen imagery in Daniel 7 and 8 (see Chapter Two above) raises anew the question as to whether astrological notions might also inform these two chapters. Dennefeld notes that in the various branches of Mesopotamian divination, "was in der einen Gattung als Omen erscheint, in der anderen Deutung ist, und umgekehrt. Die Geburtsomina sind in den astrologischen Texten des öfteren als Deutungen verwendet ..., während hingegen die Himmelserscheinungen, wie Herabfallen von Sternen, Regen, Verfinsterungen, verschiedentlich in der *izbu*-Serie als Deutungen figurieren ..." (1914, 13). Clearly, a Mesopotamian astrologer might, on the basis of his observations, predict the birth of beasts comparable to those of Daniel 7 and 8. The animals of these chapters, however, themselves *require* interpretation, and are nowhere depicted as fulfillments of previous omina. In this regard, they bear a closer resemblance to the protases of the *Šumma izbu* series than to monstrous births occasionally mentioned in apodoses belonging to the astrological texts. Nevertheless, the possibility that animal symbols in the zodiac were on occasion viewed as birth anomalies cannot be ruled out and deserves consideration.

author of Daniel. In this regard, Porteous' comments on Daniel 7 apply with equal force to exegetes of both chapters:

The question which now requires careful consideration is the extent to which we must pay heed to the possible overtones of the imagery which goes to make up the vision. In fact, if we recognize the ultimate source of the imagery which the writer employs, are we entitled to read more into the vision than the author himself does? It is quite true that the language in which the vision described in this chapter is clothed has a history and calls up in the mind of the scholar who has steeped himself in ancient religious thought and practice all kinds of suggestive associations. We may not, however, assume that the sum of these associations must have been present to the minds of those who read the composition in question or even to the man who used such imagery in his descriptions .... It will be necessary, ... to distinguish between all these associations and the actual use which the author makes of the imagery and what his readers would understand by it.[24]

We shall now discuss some semantic principles underlying various types of metaphor clusters and conclude by proposing an interpretative model which accounts for all the animals of both Daniel 7 and 8, as well as their various functional characteristics.

Metaphor clusters—some semantic principles

Metaphor clusters are founded on the principle of external analogy. To illustrate, in the case of the metaphorical expression "George is a lion," George and the lion may be thought to sustain a purely *internal* relationship, in which George is to courage, etc. as a lion is to courage, etc. Thus considered, the expression may be called an "internal" metaphor.[25] In the case of an "external" metaphor, however, "attention is shifted from what George and the lion share vis-à-vis each other (internal metaphor) to how each relates to its own proper domain. George is to men as lion is to the animals: strongest, greatest of men: strongest, greatest of the animals."[26] On the basis of this *external* analogy, it is now possible to begin the clustering process by describing other men in terms of other beasts. According to Sapir, external metaphors "may be arranged on some sort of scale. On either side of the analogy the terms will be set out in such a way that they will vary along one dimension: from smallest to biggest, from weakest to strongest, from least valuable to most valuable, etc."[27] If George, the greatest of men, is a lion, then Henry, the weakest of men, must be a mouse!

[24] Porteous 1979, 97–98.
[25] Sapir 1977, 23.
[26] Sapir 1977, 24.
[27] Sapir 1977, 23–24.

Types of metaphor clusters

As metaphor clusters evolve, they may follow one of several semantic routes. Sapir suggests four possibilities:[28]

a. *The metaphor cluster may consist of external metaphors only.* In 1 Cor 12:14–30, Paul refers to the members of the church with their various ministries as parts of the body of Christ. The analogy enables the apostle to emphasize the dignity of the weaker members (vss. 22–24) and thus the need for preserving both unity and variety in the church (vss. 14–20, 25–26). Beyond these external relationships, however, Paul makes no attempt specifically to identify the foot, the ear, the eye or the nose (vss. 15–17) with any of the particular ministries of the church (vss. 28–30).

b. *External metaphors may individually become internal metaphors.* The vision of Daniel 2 is an interesting case: the various metals comprising the image—from gold to iron mixed with clay—enable the author to depict the nations represented according to a correspondingly descending scale: "After you shall arise another kingdom *inferior* to you, and yet a third kingdom of bronze, which shall rule over all the earth" (v. 39). In addition to this external relationship, however, the image of the fourth kingdom is seen to interact directly with that of the fourth metal: "And there shall be a fourth kingdom, strong as iron, because *iron breaks to pieces and shatters all things; and like iron which crushes, it shall break and crush all these*" (v. 40).

c. *An internal metaphor may become an external metaphor in relation to one or more purely external metaphors.* Here the author of Daniel 7 might be supposed to begin with a felt internal relationship between the lion image and Babylon, the first kingdom. On this basis he then proceeds to select the other beasts representing the remaining nations, without a thought for any further internal relationship between beast and nation.

d. *An internal metaphor may become an external metaphor in relation to one or more external metaphors which, via opposition, also become internal metaphors.* To return to the hypothetical Daniel 7 illustration in (c) above: This time the process is identical except that one or more of the remaining beast images now establishes an internal relationship with the kingdom it represents, thus distinguishing that nation from Babylon the lion.

Two further possibilities should also be mentioned. These are:

e. *Internal metaphors may become external metaphors when they are simply brought together.* In this case, the author of Daniel 7 begins with the belief that there is something already specifically and innately lion-like about the first kingdom, bear-like about the second, panther-like about the

---

[28] See Sapir 1977, 25–28.

third, etc. Since the author wishes to present these kingdoms in a chronological order, he is obliged to follow a corresponding order in his presentation of the beasts in the vision.

f. *A "root metaphor" may generate external metaphors belonging to several different semantic domains.*[29] *Each external metaphor then becomes an internal metaphor in its own domain, and eventually interacts across its domain with the other external metaphors. The result of this interaction is a rich and unusually complex cluster of hybrid images or metaphors.* Pepper explains the term "root metaphor" ("basic analogy"):

> The method in principle seems to be this: A man desiring to understand the world looks about for a clue to its comprehension. He pitches upon some area of commonsense fact and tries if he cannot understand other areas in terms of this one. This original area becomes then his *basic analogy* or *root metaphor*. He describes as best he can the characteristics of this area, or, if you will, discriminates its structure. A list of its structural characteristics becomes his basic concepts of explanation and description. We call them a set of categories. In terms of these categories he proceeds to study all other areas of fact whether uncriticized or previously criticized. He undertakes to interpret all facts in terms of these categories .... Some root metaphors prove more fertile than others, have greater powers of expansion and of adjustment. These survive in comparison with the others and generate the relatively adequate world theories (italics ours).[30]

Howe describes a root metaphor ("leader") at work amongst the Cuna of San Blas, Panama.[31] Most of the Cuna live on small islands within a few hundred yards of the mainland. The following excerpts, which are taken from tape recordings of admonishments given to a newly installed chief, illustrate how initial observations drawn from the domains of fish and animals provide a basis for conceptualizing leadership in both human and astral realms:

> God put us into this world having leaders .... If there is no leader, the village cannot be maintained. The members would go just anywhere ... The place would be full of fights, everything would be wrong, if there were no chief, the maintainer of the place. All the animals have leaders, and we that much more .... In the morning when the sun has risen, the minnows (*unus*) will come around here .... You won't see just three or four minnows. The minnows come in one big group. They have a leader it's said. Their leader carries all his followers ... at sunset, the minnows will go out of our waters and back into their whirlpools. Not one minnow will stay

---

[29] We define a semantic domain as consisting of "a class of objects, all of which show at least one feature in common which differentiates them from other semantic domains. Chairs, sofas, desks, end tables, and dining tables have in common the designation *furniture*" (Tyler 1969, 8).

[30] Pepper 1942, 91–92. Black prefers the term "conceptual archetype" to "root metaphor," and defines it as a "systematic repertoire of ideas by means of which a given thinker describes, by *analogical extension*, some domain to which those ideas do not immediately and literally apply" (1962, 241).

[31] Howe 1977, 139–145.

behind. They'll go back in following their leader's word. That's the way the world is.[32]

Similar observations are then drawn from the behaviour of the *Kiplu* bird, the wild pig, and the *Kelu* fish (Jack).

The text then switches from the daily movements of animals to the daily movements of humans: As the day begins, the personified Sun, *Machi Olowaipippiler* ascends into the sky with his consort *Nan Olowaili*. She sets the women to work sweeping, while he sends the men out of the village to the mainland. He is the one who sets us to work ... one will go fishing, another will go clean out his coconut groves, another will go cut bananas, another will go hunting in the forest. They'll go forth to do any number of things. They'll go out from inside the "corral" (*kalu*).[33]

Hawkes provides a more advanced case of root metaphor which includes interaction across the domains of the external metaphors:

(In) the Medieval-Elizabethan period in Britain, it is a commonplace that the various ordered "hierarchies" existed as part of an accepted "Chain of Being," and that these were woven into the fabric of everyday life. The king was the chief of the State, with his nobles ranged under him. The Sun was chief amongst the planets, with the other planets ranged under him. The Lion was chief amongst animals, the Head was the chief element in the body, and so on. The analogical relationship between these hierarchies then becomes, as is well-known, a basis for making metaphors. The sun is the "royal" planet. The king reigns, as the Sun shines (the French metaphor *le roi soleil* comes from this source); the king can be called "Lion-hearted"; he is "head" of the "body politic" and so on.[34]

Here the root metaphor "chief" serves as a means of ordering natural, cultural and cosmic domains. Success in one domain (e.g., the State) encourages extension to yet another (e.g., the planets), and continued use of these external metaphors fosters the construction of internal relationships. The sun, for instance, is thought to "order" the planets, and they in turn "obey" the sun. The more effectively the root metaphor's connotations establish themselves *within* each domain, the greater the possibility of creating new metaphors *across* the domains. Thus, the more the sun is thought to "order" the heavens, the more brilliantly the king will "shine."

Do the animal images in Daniel stem from a root metaphor? The following observations would suggest it:

The animals of Daniel 7 and 8 seem to be the offspring of interactions that have occurred across several different domains: (1) natural (predators, horned beasts, human beings); (2) cultural (rulers/kingdoms, warriors, law court, truth, sanctuary); (3) cosmic (sea, angels, God). Thus the animals

---

[32] Howe 1977, 139–140.
[33] Howe 1977, 141.
[34] Hawkes 1972, 85.

40

may be classified in relation to (1) *predators* ("devour much flesh"—7:5); (2) *horned beasts* ("a ram ... had two horns"—8:3); (3) *human beings* ("it was lifted up from the ground and made to stand upon two feet like a man; and the mind of a man was given to it"—7:4; "as for the rest of the beasts, their dominion was taken away ... there came one like a son of man ... And to him was given dominion"—7:12–14); (4) *rulers/kingdoms* ("These four great beasts are four kings"—7:17; "As for the fourth beast, there shall be a fourth kingdom on earth"—7:23); (5) *warriors* ("the horn made war with the saints"—7:21); (6) *the law court* ("As for the rest of these beasts, their dominion was taken away"—7:12); (7) *the truth* ("truth was cast down to the ground"—8:12); (8) *the sanctuary* ("the place of his sanctuary was overthrown"—8:11); (9) *the sea* ("four great beasts came up out of the sea"—7:3); (10) *the angels (saints, stars)*[35] ("this horn made war with the saints"—7:21; "some of the host of the stars it cast down to the ground and trampled upon them"—8:10; "it magnified itself, even to the Prince of the host"—8:11); (11) *God* ("one that was ancient of days took his seat"—7:9).

Hybrid images of this sort have long been recognized as characteristic of apocalyptic. They are also quite comparable to Hawkes' examples of domain-crossing in Medieval-Elizabethan Britain: a *lion*-hearted *king* who *shines as the sun* over the *body politic* would be quite at home in the book of Daniel!

Since the animals of Daniel 7 and 8 betray characteristics relating to at least eleven different domains, a fruitful line of inquiry might proceed according to the following hypothesis: A root metaphor taken from the world of predators and horned beasts has generated new external metaphors in each of these domains. These external metaphors have in turn established internal relationships *within* their respective domains, and then, by interacting *across* these domains, produced the functional hybrids described in the two chapters. Finally, two additional factors might be suggested as having guided in the actual selection of images for the visions from the virtually unlimited number of possible combinations at hand: (1) the historical circumstances giving rise to the visions (e.g., attack on temple and community, expectation of judgment); and (2) the availability to the author of traditional image combinations.

Conclusion

In this chapter, we considered the functional characteristics of the animals of Daniel 7 and 8 and introduced the notion of a metaphor cluster. Several

---

[35] For the identification of the saints and the stars with angels in Daniel 7 and 8, see Collins 1977, 123–147.

attempts to organize the animal images according to clusters were then reviewed, and their limitations noted. We then set out to develop an interpretative model for a metaphor cluster of a more comprehensive nature, and concluded by proposing a "root metaphor"-type model which might account for the particular animals of both chapters, their various functional characteristics, as well as their suitability as political symbols.

CHAPTER 4

Daniel 7 and 8 and the Animal Apocalypse

Introduction

In the previous chapter, we proposed a "root metaphor"-type model to describe how the animal images of Daniel 7 and 8 might function as a metaphor cluster involving at least eleven different domains. In the present chapter, we shall argue that the root metaphor informing these domains is that of the shepherd. We shall arrive at this conclusion by noting that in the contemporaneous Animal Apocalypse of 1 Enoch 85–90,[1] no fewer than nine of the eleven domains found in Daniel 7 and 8 are informed by the shepherd metaphor.

Preliminary considerations

The Animal Apocalypse of 1 Enoch 85–90 presents a "zoomorphic" history extending from the creation of Adam to the final advent of God's kingdom. Nations and individuals are depicted as various animals—the patriarchs by bulls and the faithful of later times by sheep. Israel's oppressors are symbolized by wild beasts and birds of prey, the fallen Watchers are stars, while the unfallen angels are depicted as men. God is frequently referred to as "the Lord of the sheep." Although exegetes over the years have repeatedly pointed to this work as a potential key to the symbolic language of Daniel,[2] surprisingly little has been done to pursue this possibility in a

---

[1] All citations from 1 Enoch are according to Knibb, 1978.

[2] Rowley 1944, 58: "[In the Animal Apocalypse], the use of the figures of sheep and bulls, and of horns, to symbolize men ... and the thought of the final great assault on the Jews, followed by the destruction of their foes and the resurrection of the righteous, closely resembles what we find in Daniel." Dexinger 1969, 24: "Ein richtiges Verständnis für die literarische Art der Visionen bei Daniel ist ohne Berücksichtigung der ausserkanonischen apokalyptischen Literatur nicht möglich. Besonders aufschlussreich ist in diesem Zusammenhang ein Hinweis auf die Kapitel 83–90 des äthiopischen Henochbuches." Collins 1976, 214: "The similarity of the four beasts in Daniel 7, representing four kingdoms ranging from Babylon to the Seleucids, to the seventy shepherds in the Animal Apocalypse is evident." Knibb 1976, 256: "In the Vision of the Animals (1 Enoch 85–90) ... the use of animals to represent human beings was probably directly influenced by the symbolism of Daniel 7 and 8, ... In its details the Vision of the Animals seems in many ways to reflect the same attitude as the book of Daniel." Hartman and di Lella 1978, 92: "the Book of Dreams [is] a potentially important source for determining the meaning of the symbolism in Daniel 7."

systematic way.[3] Important similarities in the form, structure and historico-cultural context of both works invite comparison of the animal imagery:

a. The Animal Apocalypse, like Daniel 7 and 8, is an apocalyptic allegory of history.[4] As such, it reviews events of the past from the purported prophetic standpoint of an earlier visionary, only to concentrate on the author's own age and his expectations of the imminent end-time.

b. Thus, as in Daniel 7 and 8, the vision-report formula "I saw" frequently punctuates the Animal Apocalypse (1 En 85:1, 3, 9; 86:1, 2, 3; 87:1 etc; 88:1 etc; Dan 7:2, 7 cf. vss. 4, 5, 6, 8, 9, 11, 21; 8:2, 3, 4, 7 etc).

c. Whereas Dan 9:24–27 reinterprets the seventy years of exile (Jer 25:11; 29:10–14) as seventy weeks of years reaching to the inauguration of the eschatological era, the Animal Apocalypse describes the period from the exile to the end-time in terms of seventy shepherds who individually are assigned a fixed time-span and are held responsible for the fate of the people of God (1 En 89:59–90:25).[5]

d. These seventy shepherds are divided into four groups. The first group of twelve is responsible for the period from the conquest of the northern kingdom to the return from exile under Cyrus (89:65–71); the second group of twenty-three shepherds covers the Persian period (89:72–77); the period from Alexander to the end of Ptolemaic control of Palestine is represented by a further twenty-three shepherds (90:1–5), and another twelve are apportioned the period from the beginning of Seleucid control of Palestine until the final judgment (90:6–17). This arbitrary division of Israel's history reflects the idea of four world empires preceding the eschatological era (cf. Daniel 2 and 7),[6] an idea which places both the Animal Apocalypse and Daniel in the realm of Near-Eastern resistance literature.[7]

e. As in Daniel 7 and 8, the main emphasis in the Book of Dreams falls on the Seleucid period (1 En 90:5ff).[8] This section is of particular importance

---

[3] Beer (1900, 290) and Collins (1974b, 61–62) sought to identify the son of man of Daniel 7 as an angel on the basis of the symbolism of men representing angels in the Animal Apocalypse. See also Charles 1929, 187.

[4] Eissfeldt 1974, 56.

[5] Knibb 1976, 256.

[6] Milik 1976, 254; Knibb 1976, 256–257.

[7] Cf. Collins 1977, 207. The division of the number 70 into groups of 12, 23, 23 and 12 is of interest. This particular breakdown suggests a fusion of the traditional fourfold division of history with an attempt to divide 70 into three groups of 23. Two passages in the book of Daniel also suggest an interest in the number 23 in relation to the end-time. In Dan 8:14, the temple is restored after the completion of 2300 (23×100) evenings and mornings, while in 9:25–26, 69 (23×3) weeks of years precede the final seventieth week which marks the *terminus ad quem* of the time given for the completion of the new temple and its dedication (9:24).

[8] Knibb 1976, 258.

because it indicates the historical background of the work. The writer's sympathies are with the Hasidim, who are symbolized by the lambs born to the white sheep (90:6–7). 90:8 depicts the murder of Onias in the summer of 170 BCE. The horned lambs (90:9) symbolize the Maccabees, and the great horn in the same verse represents Judas Maccabaeus.[9] Since the great horn continues to fight until the end of the dominion of the last twelve shepherds (90:16), this section was written sometime after Mattathias was succeeded by Judas (166/165 BCE), but sometime before the latter's death in 161 BCE.[10] Milik believes the work was composed in the early months of 164 BCE, during the weeks following the battle of Bethsur described in 1 En 90:13–15.[11] Since it is not known how many weeks or months either Daniel or the Animal Apocalypse was in the making, it is sufficient to date both works generally within the period 167–164 BCE. It can, therefore, be reasonably assumed that the Animal Apocalypse represents the work of a Hasid who was writing within one or two years of the author of Daniel, and hence under largely identical historical circumstances.[12]

Although it is frequently argued that the author of Daniel was himself a Hasid,[13] reference to the "little help" in Dan 11:34 indicates a far less supportive attitude towards the Maccabees than does the eschatological role afforded the great horn Judas in 1 Enoch 90. Whereas a great sword features prominently in the Animal Apocalypse (90:19), national liberation according to Daniel is to be secured "by no human hand" (Dan 8:25 cf. 2:45). Consequently, Daniel is generally considered to represent the views of a pacifist circle within the Hasidic movement, although evidence for the existence of such a circle at this time is lacking.[14] In any case, both the Animal Apocalypse and Daniel may be classified as resistance tracts, designed to inspire their readers to pursue military and non-military options respectively in the Holy War against the Syrian oppressor.[15]

f. Thus, like Daniel, the author of the Animal Apocalypse awaits the intervention of Michael (90:14, 17 cf. Dan 12:1),[16] the destruction of the Syrians (90:12 cf. Dan 7:26; 8:25; 11:45), the final judgment (90:20 cf. Dan 7:9–10), the new temple (90:29 cf. Dan 8:14; 9:24), and the resurrection of

---

[9] According to most modern exegetes.

[10] Charles (ed.) 1913, 2:170–171.

[11] Milik 1976, 44.

[12] Attempts to date the Animal Apocalypse under John Hyrcanus (134–103 BCE) (Stern 1961, 1–22) or Alexander Jannaeus (103–76 BCE) (Torrey 1954, 208–211; Zeitlin 1961–62, 1–33) have few modern supporters.

[13] More recently, Hartman and di Lella 1978, 43–45.

[14] Collins 1977, 214.

[15] Collins 1977, 205–210.

[16] Hengel 1974, 1:188.

the persecuted faithful (90:33 cf. Dan 12:2). Such hopes and aspirations indicate a common religious sentiment animating Jewish nationalists of the time. [17]

Literary criticism of the Animal Apocalypse

Before we proceed to compare the animal imagery of Daniel with that of the Animal Apocalypse, two literary-critical problems relative to the latter work require consideration.

a. The Animal Apocalypse has been criticized as a "ziemlich geschmack-lose Allegorie," [18] which is "mostly external and clumsy." [19] A common cause for complaint is that the same animals are frequently used to represent different historical referents. For example, in 1 Enoch 89 alone, Jacob, his twelve sons, Moses, Aaron, Joshua, Caleb, Saul, Samuel, David, Elijah, Zerubbabel, Joshua and either Ezra or Nehemiah are alike referred to as sheep or rams. Similarly, wild boars represent the Edomites in 89:66 and the Samaritans in 89:72. In 90:2, vultures and kites symbolize the Egyptians, but probably refer to Ammon and Moab in 90:13. Di Lella finds here a "confused and confusing symbolism" which must be classified as "multireferential symbolism of a rather pedestrian sort." [20]

The very fact, however, that the author of the Animal Apocalypse refuses to invent new animals in order to accommodate additional referents testifies to the importance of the pastoral metaphor underlying his work. The allegory is no more "geschmacklos" or "pedestrian" than the herding world in which it moves. [21]

b. A more serious problem affecting the interpretation of metaphor in the Animal Apocalypse is the apparent intrusion of the primary subject into the narrative, which is purportedly symbolic (90:41). In 86:6, for example, men are not referred to as animals but are simply called "the sons of the earth." Similarly, in 89:1, Noah "was born a bull, but became a man, and built for himself a large vessel and dwelt on it." In 89:6, sinners destroyed in the

---

[17] Naturally, certain differences also characterize these two works. The Animal Apocalypse begins with the creation, and includes the theme of the fall of the Watchers. Several scholars note a certain antagonism towards the second temple in 1 En 89:73, which is without parallel in the book of Daniel. Similarly, no clear reference is made to Antiochus' "abomination of desolation" in the Animal Apocalypse.

[18] Beer 1900, 289.

[19] Flusser 1971, 1199.

[20] Hartman and di Lella 1978, 93.

[21] Reference to elephants and various wild beasts in 86:4 and 89:10 reflects birth-omen notions (see Chapter Two), and should not be dismissed as a naive literary device to accommodate additional historical referents.

Deluge are depicted as "bulls and elephants and camels and asses," while the animals destroyed with them are simply referred to as "all the animals."[22] Again, in 86:1, the fallen angels are depicted as stars which pasture among the bulls, yet these same stars are bound by their hands and feet in 88:3 (cf. Azazel in 10:4). In 89:15–16, certain sheep "complain" to God, and cry out for help. Finally, in 90:31, a ram extends his "hand" to take hold of Enoch, (even though in the following verse reference is made to white sheep with thick and pure wool), and in 90:19, a large sword is given to the sheep.

This tendency apparently to defy the rules of good symbolic narrative probably stems from a particular mentality rather than from poor literary taste. For the author and his contemporaries, many of his animal metaphors might have reflected a perceived kinship between man and beast approaching literal identification. Examples of figurative language based on identification have been noted in both Mesopotamian and OT texts. According to van Dijk, "Die literarischen Vergleiche der Sumerer sind vielfach Identifikationen, keine Analogien."[23] The same has been said of the animal comparisons of Genesis 49 and Deuteronomy 33, which Gunneweg regards as dynamic identifications, since they seek to ascribe to the tribe thus compared the powers or characteristics of the animal described.[24]

Animal identification in an Israelite milieu is readily conceivable in the light of the nation's pastoralist origins. For a shepherd who knew all his sheep by name, who spent the major part of his life caring for them, talking to them and observing (with no small satisfaction) that they responded to his voice alone (cf. John 10:3–5), the step of attributing a quasi-human status to such animals would have been a relatively natural one. Such a background probably accounts for the high social position attributed to animals in the OT.[25] Animal and human souls were of the same kind (Gen 1:20–21 cf. 2:7). As man's fellow creatures, animals observed the sabbath (Ex 20:10; Deut 5:14), were shipmates with Noah in the ark, and were parties with Noah to God's covenant (Gen 9:9–10). In the book of Jonah, mention is made of a public lament involving man and beast alike (3:7–8), and the prayers of both reach the ear of God (4:11).[26] According to Nathan's parable, a lamb might be adopted as a member of the family, while David views the murder of this

---

[22] Cf. Hartman and di Lella 1978, 93.
[23] van Dijk 1971, 439.
[24] Gunneweg 1964, 245–255.
[25] Armstrong 1981, 35.
[26] Cf. Hambly 1937, 1:350: "Among the Bayankole ... when a king dies, his body is wrapped in the hide of a newly killed cow, after the royal corpse has been washed with milk ... and even the cattle are made to participate in the mourning. Cows are separated from their calves so that both make a melancholy lowing."

lamb as a capital offence (2 Sam 12:1–5).[27] Sometimes the OT ascribes moral guilt to animals. In Gen 9:5, for example, both man and beast are accountable to God for the shedding of blood. Similarly, Leviticus 20 places equal blame on man and animal in cases of unnatural union between the two (vss. 15–16). The notion lingers on in the Mischna (Sanhedrin 1.4), where the council of twenty-three is responsible for deciding on such cases:

A beast that commits or suffers unnatural crime [is judged] by three and twenty, ...
The wolf, the lion, the bear, the leopard, the panther, or serpent [that have killed a man], their death [is decided upon] by three and twenty [judges].[28]

It is, therefore, quite possible that in the Animal Apocalypse with its underlying pastoral metaphor, notions of beasts representing individuals, beasts crying out to God, or even beasts coming into judgment (see below), indicate in the first place a particular mentality capable of some sort of literal identification rather than mere analogy. This, of course, is not to deny that the author also sees a very real analogy between his allegory and the historical facts of Israel's existence. Identification and analogy are by no means mutually exclusive, and the suggestion is simply that in the OT world, the former naturally gave rise to the latter.

Animal imagery in Daniel and the Animal Apocalypse

We shall now examine the animal images of Daniel 7 and 8 against the pastoral world brought to view in the Animal Apocalypse. As the following parallels indicate, nine of the eleven domains already noted in connection with the animals of Daniel also occur in the latter work. These are (1) predators; (2) horned beasts; (3) human beings; (4) rulers/kingdoms; (5) warriors; (6) law court; (7) temple; (8) angels; (9) God.

1. Predators

Anomalous predators:

Dan 7:4–6	1 En 89:55; 90:2
The first was like a *lion* and had eagles' wings ...	And he gave them into the hands of the *lions* and the *tigers* and

---

[27] Cf. Frankfort 1978, 164–165: "In Uganda 'men become warmly attached to their cows; some of them they love like children, pet and talk to them, and weep over their ailments. Should a favorite cow die, their grief is extreme and cases are not wanting in which men have committed suicide through excessive grief at the loss of an animal.' In the same region 'a chief will frequently bemoan the loss of one of his cows with more genuine and heartfelt grief than he would display if he lost a wife or a child.'"
[28] Danby 1933, 383.

And behold, another beast, a
second one, like a *bear*. It
was raised up on one side ...
After this I looked, and lo,
another, like a *leopard*, with
four wings of a bird on its
back ...

the *wolves* and the *hyenas*, and
into the hands of the *foxes*, and
to all the animals; and those
wild animals began to tear those
sheep in pieces ...
And after this I saw in the vision
all the birds of heaven coming:
the *eagles*, and the *vultures*,
and the *kites*, and the *ravens*;
but the eagles led all the birds;
and they began to devour those
sheep, and to peck out their eyes,
and to devour their flesh.

(That the above animals are birth
anomalies is indicated in 89:10:
"And they [the bulls] began to
beget wild animals and birds,
so that there arose from them
every kind of species: *lions,
tigers, wolves,* dogs, *hyenas,*
wild-boars, *foxes,* badgers, pigs,
falcons, *vultures, kites, eagles*
and *ravens*").

2. Horned beasts

a. Rams:

Dan 8:3

I raised my eyes and saw, and
behold, a *ram* standing on the
bank of the river ...

1 En 89:28, 42, 45, 46, 48

And I saw the Lord of the sheep
pasturing them and giving them
water and grass, and that sheep
going and leading them ...
until the Lord of the sheep
raised up a *ram* from among them
which led them ...
And the Lord of the sheep sent
the sheep to another sheep and
raised it up to be a *ram*, and
to lead the sheep in place of
that sheep which had renounced
its glory.
And it went to it, and spoke with
it alone, and raised up that *ram*,
and made it the prince and leader
of the sheep ...
And that second *ram* rose up and
led the small sheep, and that
ram begat many sheep and fell
asleep; and a small sheep became

ram in place of it, and became
the prince and leader of those
sheep.

b. Ram versus ram or goat:

Dan 8:5–6

As I was considering, behold,
a he-goat came from the west ...
he came to the ram with the
two horns ... and he ran at him
in his mighty wrath.

1 En 89:47

And the first ram pursued that
second ram, and that second ram
rose and fled before it.

c. Single ram defeats beasts:

Dan 8:4

I saw the ram charging (LXX κερατίςοντα)
westward and northward and southward;
no beast could stand before him ...

1 En 89:43, 49

And that ram began to butt
(Vat. κερατίςειν) those dogs and
foxes and wild boars, on one side
and on the other, until it had
destroyed them all ...
and that ram butted and killed all
the animals, and those animals did
not again prevail amongst the
sheep and did not seize anything
further from them.

d. Ram (not) rescued from enemy seeking to break its horn(s):

Dan 8:7

I saw him come close to the ram,
and he was enraged against him
and struck the ram and broke
his two horns; and the ram had
no power to stand before him,
but he cast him down to the
ground and trampled upon him;
and there was no one who could
rescue the ram from his power.

1 En 90:13–14

And I looked at them until the
shepherds and the eagles and
those vultures and kites came
and cried to the ravens that
they should dash the horn of that
ram in pieces; and they fought
and battled with it, and it fought
with them and cried out that its
help might come to it.
And I looked until that man who wrote
down the names of the shepherds
and brought (them) up before
the Lord of the sheep came, and
he helped that ram and showed it
everything, (namely, that) its
help was coming down.

e. Unicorn:

Dan 8:5

As I was considering, behold,

1 En 90:9

And I looked until horns came

a he-goat came from the west
across the face of the whole
earth, without touching the
ground; and the goat had a
conspicuous horn between his
eyes.

up on those lambs, but the ravens
cast their horns down; and I
looked until a big horn grew
on one of those sheep, and their
eyes were opened.

f. Horned beasts that bite with their teeth:

Dan 7:7

After this I saw in the night
visions, and behold, a fourth
beast, terrible and dreadful
and exceedingly strong; and it
had great iron teeth ... and it
had ten horns.

1 En 86:5

and they began to bite with
their teeth, and to devour,
and to gore with their horns.

g. Horns noted for their size:

Dan 7:20; 8:3, 5, 8, 9, 10

the other horn ... which
seemed *greater than its
fellows* ...
it had two horns; and *both
horns were high*, but one was
higher than the other, and the
higher one came up last ...
and the goat had *a conspicuous
horn* between his eyes ...
there came up four *conspicuous
horns* ...
a little horn, *which grew
exceedingly great* ...
it grew *great* ...

1 En 90:9, 37, 38

I looked until *a big horn* grew
on one of those sheep ...
And I saw how a white bull was
born, and *its horns were big* ...
and that wild-ox was a large
animal and had *big black horns*
on its head.

h. Horns seen to grow in the vision:

Dan 7:8; 8:3, 8, 9, 10

I considered the horns, and
behold, there *came up* among
them another horn ...
the higher one *came up* last ...
instead of it there *came up*
four conspicuous horns ...
out of one of them *came forth*
a little horn, which *grew*
exceedingly great ...
it *grew* great ...

1 En 90:9

And I looked until horns *came
up* on those lambs ... and I
looked until a big horn *grew*
on one of those sheep ...

51

i. Single horn precipitating the end-time:

Dan 7:8–10; 8:12, 13

I considered the horns, and
behold, there came up among
them another horn ...
and behold, in this horn were
eyes like the eyes of a man,
and a mouth speaking great
things.
As I looked, thrones were
placed and one that was ancient
of days took his seat ...
the court sat in judgment, and
the books were opened ...
and the horn acted and
prospered.
Then I heard a holy one speaking; and another holy one said
to the one that spoke, For how
long ...?

1 En 90:16–20

All the eagles and vultures and
ravens and kites gathered together and brought with them
all the wild sheep, and
they all came together and
helped one another in order to
dash that horn of the ram in
pieces.
And I looked at that man who
wrote the book at the command
of the Lord until he opened
that book of the destruction
which those twelve last
shepherds had wrought, and he
showed before the Lord of the
sheep that they had destroyed
even more than (those) before
them.
And I looked until the Lord of
the sheep came to them and
took in his hand the staff of
his anger ...
And I looked until a big sword
was given to the sheep ...
And I looked until a throne was
set up in the pleasant land,
and the Lord of the sheep sat
on it; and they took all the
sealed books and opened those
books before the Lord of the
sheep.

j. Broken horns:

Dan 8:7, 8, 22

he ... struck the ram and
broke his two horns ...
the great horn was *broken* ...
as for the horn that was
broken ...

1 En 90:9, 12, 13, 16

And I looked until horns came
up on those lambs, but the ravens
cast their horns down ...
And those ravens battled and
fought with it, and wished *to
make away with its horn*, but
they did not prevail against
it.
And I looked at them until the
shepherds and the eagles and
those vultures and kites came
and cried to the ravens that

they should *dash the horn of
that ram in pieces* ...
All the eagles and vultures and
ravens and kites gathered together and brought with them
all the wild sheep, and they
all came together and helped
one another in order to *dash
that horn of the ram in pieces.*

3. Human beings

Beasts transformed into human beings:

Dan 7:4

The first was like a lion and
had eagles' wings. Then as I
looked its wings were plucked off,
and it was lifted up from the
ground and made to stand upon
two feet like a man; and the mind
of a man was given to it.

1 En 89:1, 36

He was born a bull,[29] but became
a man, and built for himself a
large vessel and dwelt on it ...
And I looked there at the vision
until that sheep became a man,
and built a house for the Lord
of the sheep.

Charles[30] thinks the bull and the sheep (Noah and Moses) in the Animal
Apocalypse are changed into men in order to perform a man's task of
building. However, in 1 En 89:72, three sheep rebuild a house without
becoming men. Here it is useful to compare 1 En 90:38, where all the
animals are transformed into white bulls, which obviously represents a
return to conditions during the *Urzeit* (cf. chapter 85). This allows the
inference that transformation in the Animal Apocalypse is symbolic rather
than mechanical. Elsewhere in the Animal Apocalypse, men represent angels (89:59, 61 cf. 90:22). Since angels build the ark in 67:2, it is probable that
89:1 alludes to this tradition by having Noah transformed into a man when
he builds the ark. A similar tradition regarding angelic construction of the
tabernacle might be supposed.

4. Rulers, kingdoms

Beasts representing rulers or kingdoms:

Dan 7:17, 23; 8:20

These four great beasts are four
kings who shall arise out of the

(1 En 89:55; 90:2); 89:28, 42, 45, 46, 48

(89:55; 90:2): Charles identifies
the lions and tigers as the

---

[29] Mention of Noah's transformation from a bull to a man does not occur in the Aramaic
fragment 4QEn^e4i. See Milik 1976, 238–239.
[30] Charles (ed.) 1913, 2:251, 253.

earth ...
As for the fourth beast, there
shall be a fourth kingdom ...

As for the ram which you saw
with the two horns, these are
the kings of Media and Persia.

Assyrians and Babylonians, the
wolves as the Egyptians, and
the hyenas as perhaps the
Ethiopians. The eagles are the
Greeks or Macedonians, the ravens
the Syrians under the Seleucidae,
and the vultures and kites are
the Egyptians under the Ptolemies.[31]

And I saw the Lord of the sheep
pasturing them and giving them
water and grass, and that sheep
going and leading them ...
until the Lord of the sheep raised
up a ram from among them which
led them ...
And the Lord of the sheep sent
the sheep to another sheep and
raised it up to be a ram, and
to lead the sheep in place of
that sheep which had renounced
its glory.
And it went to it, and spoke
with it alone, and raised up that
ram, and made it the prince and
leader of the sheep ...
And that second ram rose up and
led the small sheep, and that
ram begat many sheep and fell
asleep; and a small sheep became
ram in place of it, and became
the prince and leader of those
sheep.

5. Warriors

Beasts representing warriors:

Dan 7:21
As I looked, this horn made war
with the saints, and prevailed
over them

1 En 90:19
And I looked until a big sword
was given to the sheep, and the
sheep went out against all the
wild animals to kill them ...

---

[31] Charles (ed.) 1913, 2:255, 257.

6. Law court

a. Judgment from books of record:

Dan 7:9–10

As I looked, *thrones were placed* and one that was ancient of days *took his seat*; his raiment was white as snow, and the hair of his head like pure wool ... the court sat in judgment, and *the books were opened.*

1 En 90:20

And I looked until *a throne was set up* in the pleasant land, and the Lord of the sheep *sat on it*; and they took all the sealed books and *opened those books* before the Lord of the sheep.

b. Fiery judgment of beasts:

Dan 7:10, 11

a stream of fire issued and came forth from before him ... And as I looked, *the beast was slain, and its body destroyed and given over to be burned with fire.*

1 En 90:24–27

And the judgment was held first on the stars, and they were judged and found guilty; and they went to the place of damnation, and were thrown into a deep (place), *full of fire, burning and full of pillars of fire.*
And those seventy shepherds were judged and found guilty, and they also were thrown into that *abyss of fire.*
And I saw at that time how a similar abyss was opened in the middle of the earth which was *full of fire*, and they brought those blind sheep, and they were all judged and found guilty and thrown into that *abyss of fire, and they burned*; and that abyss was on the south of that house. *And I saw those sheep burning, and their bones were burning.*

7. Temple

a. Temple attacked by beasts:

Dan 8:9, 11, 13

Out of one of them came forth a little horn ... It magnified itself, even up to the Prince of the host; and the continual burnt

1 En 89:66–67

And the lions and the tigers devoured and swallowed up the majority of those sheep, and the wild boars devoured with them; and *they burnt down that tower*

offering was taken away from him, and *the place of his sanctuary was overthrown* ... For how long is the vision concerning ... the giving over of the *sanctuary and host to be trampled under foot?*

and demolished that house. And I was extremely sad about the tower, because that house of the sheep had been demolished; and after that I was unable to see whether those sheep went into that house.

b. Temple in "glorious land":

Dan 8:9, 11

Out of one of them came forth a little horn, which grew exceedingly great toward the south, toward the east, and toward the *glorious land* ... the place of his *sanctuary* was overthrown.

1 En 89:40

And I looked until the sheep came to a good place and *a pleasant and glorious land*, and I looked until those sheep were satisfied; and that *house* (was) in the middle of them in the *pleasant land*.

c. New temple:

Dan 8:14

And he said to him, For two thousand and three hundred evenings and mornings; then *the sanctuary shall be restored to its rightful state.*

1 En 90:29

And I looked until the Lord of the sheep brought *a new house*, larger and higher than that first one, and *he set it up* on the site of the first one which had been folded up; and *all its pillars were new*, and its ornaments (were) new and larger than (those of) the first one, the old one which he had removed. And the Lord of the sheep was in the middle of it.

Volz[32] and more recently Gaston[33] have argued that the "new house" in 1 En 90:29 stands for Jerusalem only and not for the temple. This is because both the first and second temples are already depicted under the image of a tower, which is built in addition to the house (Jerusalem) (89:50, 56, 72, 73). Since no tower is mentioned in connection with the new house in 90:29, their conclusion is that the vision depicts a new Jerusalem without a temple at the end-time. In reply to Volz, Schrenk[34] remarks, "But there is no Jerusalem without the temple," an argument which Gaston thinks simply begs the question. Significantly, Gaston himself wishes to argue that the removal of

---

[32] Volz 1934, 217.
[33] Gaston 1970, 114.
[34] Schrenk 1965, 240.

the "old house" in 90:28 implies not only the destruction of the old Jerusalem, but more specifically of its temple, even though here also no mention is made of the tower. This is because the removal of the old house seems to be an act of judgment on the second temple, which, according to 89:73, was polluted.[35] Gaston cannot have it both ways. If the removal of the old house implies the destruction of the old temple, then there is no prima facie reason for denying a new temple when the new house is established. Compare already 89:36, where the tabernacle in the wilderness is depicted as "a house for the Lord of the sheep." Any reference to Jerusalem here is quite impossible.

8. *Angels*

a. Stars depicted as sheep or cattle:

Dan 8:10

It grew great even to the host of heaven, and some of the host of the stars its cast down to the ground, and trampled upon them.

1 En 86:1

And again I looked with my eyes as I was sleeping, and I saw heaven above, and behold, a star fell from heaven, and it arose and ate and pastured amongst those bulls.

As noted already in Chapter Three, the stars in Dan 8:10 are treated in the same way as is the ram in 8:7, which is "cast ... down to the ground and trampled upon" by the he-goat. (For discussion of "truth" and the sanctuary, which are similarly "cast down to the ground" or "trampled under foot" (Dan 8:11, 12, 13), see Chapter Five).

b. Men representing angels:

Dan 8:15, 16

there stood before me *one having the appearance of a man.*
And I heard a man's voice between the banks of the Ulai, and it called, *Gabriel*, make this man understand the vision.

1 En 87:2; 90:21, 22

And I raised my eyes again to heaven and saw in the vision, and behold, there came from heaven *beings who were like white men*; and four came from that place, and three (others) with them ...
And the Lord called *those men, the seven first white ones* ...
And he said to *that man who wrote before him, who was one of the seven white ones*—he said to him: Take those seventy shepherds ...

---

[35] Gaston 1970, 114.

In 1 Enoch 20, seven holy angels are mentioned by name: Uriel, Raphael, Raguel, Michael, Saraqael, *Gabriel* (cf. Dan 8:16) and Remiel.

c. Patron angels depicted as shepherds:

Dan 8:10, 11	*1 En 89:59*
some of the host of the stars it cast down to the ground, and trampled upon them. It magnified itself, even up to the Prince of the host ...	And he called seventy shepherds and cast off those sheep that they might pasture them.

The "Prince of the host" in Dan 8:11 is probably "Michael, the great prince" who intercedes for Israel in Dan 12:1.[36] Since the host or stars belonging to the Prince are depicted as sheep or cattle (see above), Michael, or the Prince of the host, is their leader or shepherd.

The seventy shepherds of 1 En 89:59 represent the patron angels of the seventy nations.[37] This is because in 89:61, the heavenly scribe is referred to as "another," (presumably another shepherd *vis-à-vis* the seventy), while in 90:22, this same heavenly scribe is identified as "one of the seven white ones," i.e., one of the angels. Similarly, Plato (*Politicus* 271 d/e and *Critias* 109 b/c) mentions patron shepherd daemons or gods, while in the Heb Test Napht 8:3–6, reference is made to "seventy ministering angels, Michael at their head," who are commanded "to teach the seventy families which sprang from the loins of Noah seventy languages."[38]

d. Israel's patron angel secures deliverance at opening of books of record:

Dan 12:1	*1 En 90:14, 17, 18*
At that time shall arise Michael, the great prince who has charge of your people. And there shall be a time of trouble, such as never has been since there was a nation till that time; but at that time *your people shall be delivered, every one whose name shall be found written in the book.*	And I looked until that man who wrote down the names of the shepherds and brought (them) up before the Lord of the sheep came, and *he helped that ram* and showed it everything, (namely, that) its help was coming down ... And I looked at *that man who wrote the book at the command of the Lord until he opened that book* of the destruction which those twelve last shepherds had wrought, and *he showed before the Lord of the sheep* that they had destroyed

---

[36] Cf. Lacocque 1979, 162.
[37] So most exegetes.
[38] Charles (ed.) 1913, 2:363.

even more than (those) before
them.
And I looked until the Lord of
the sheep came to them and took
in his hand the staff of his
anger and struck the earth; and
the earth was split, and all
the animals and the birds of
heaven fell from those sheep and
sank in the earth, and it closed
over them.

9. *God*

a. Judges beasts:

Dan 7:9–12

one that was ancient of
days took his seat ...
the books were opened ...
the beast was slain and its
body destroyed ...
as for the rest of the beasts,
their dominion was taken
away ...

1 En 90:17–18, 26

And I looked at that man who
wrote the book at the command
of the Lord until he opened that
book of the destruction which
those twelve last shepherds had
wrought, and he showed before
the Lord of the sheep that they
had destroyed even more than
(those) before them.
And I looked until the Lord of
the sheep came to them and
took in his hand the staff of
his anger and struck the earth;
and the earth was split, and
all the animals and the birds
of heaven fell from those sheep
and sank in the earth, and it
closed over them ...
and they brought those blind
sheep, and they were all judged
and found guilty ...

b. Restores temple:

Dan 8:13–14

For how long ...? ...
then the sanctuary shall be
restored to its rightful state.

1 En 90:29

And I looked until the Lord of
the sheep brought a new house ...

In Dan 8:13–14, the sanctuary is probably restored by God, since in the OT,
the lament formula "How long?" is traditionally a call for divine intervention, while the passive construction "then the sanctuary shall be restored to

its rightful state" may be best understood as a circumlocution of the divine name ("divine passive").[39]

Conclusion

Our proposal was that a root metaphor taken from the world of predators and horned beasts has informed the numerous domains noted in Daniel 7 and 8 (natural, cultural and cosmic). In the present chapter, we have tested this hypothesis by comparing Daniel 7 and 9 with a contemporaneous apocalyptic work (the Animal Apocalypse), whose animal imagery is clearly informed by the world of the shepherd. We have advanced twenty-five specific parallels relative to the animal imagery of both works, and have noted that no fewer than nine of the eleven domains identified in Daniel 7 and 8 also occur in the Animal Apocalypse. These results, we believe, indicate that the animal metaphors of Daniel 7 and 8 find their origin in the root metaphor of the shepherd.

[39] Cf. Jeremias (1971, 13): "the 'divine passive' ... occurs frequently for the first time in the book of the prophet Daniel."

CHAPTER 5

Daniel 7 and 8 and the OT lamentation literature

Introduction

Having compared Daniel 7 and 8 with a contemporaneous apocalyptic work (the Animal Apocalypse), we shall now examine these chapters in the light of their OT and ancient Near Eastern backgrounds. From this perspective, it will be argued that the root metaphor "shepherd," mediated by the office of the king,[1] has generated external metaphors in all eleven of the semantic domains relative to the beasts of Daniel 7 and 8. We shall indicate various internal relationships evident within these respective domains, and suggest how interactions across the domains account for the functional characteristics of the animals described in these two chapters. In addition, it will be argued that the shepherd metaphor also accounts for the animals' physical peculiarities discussed in Part II of this study.

Our thesis is that the root metaphor "shepherd" has generated the following external metaphors informing Daniel 7 and 8: (1) The herd leader is the SHEPHERD of the flock; (2) The military leader is the SHEPHERD of the warriors; (3) The warrior is the (destructive) SHEPHERD of the enemy; (4) The ruler is the SHEPHERD of the nation; (5) God/Michael is the SHEPHERD of the angels; (6) The ruler is the SHEPHERD of the temple; (7) God is the SHEPHERD of truth; (8) The judge is the SHEPHERD of the oppressed; (9) The predator is the (destructive) SHEPHERD of the oppressed; (10) The man is the SHEPHERD of the animals; (11) The storm god is the SHEPHERD of the flock; (12) God is the SHEPHERD of Israel.

Evidence for these external metaphors will be found primarily in the OT lamentation literature, which, we shall argue, provides an important source for the animal imagery of Daniel 7 and 8.

OT lamentation literature and the visions of Daniel

An obvious point of contact between the Daniel visions and the OT lamentation literature is the lament formula "How long?" which climaxes the

---

[1] References to divine beings as "shepherds" in this context are taken as projections of the king's office on to the heavenly realm. Cf. our conclusion to this chapter.

visions of chapter 8 (8:13) and chapters 10–12 (12:6) by introducing cryptic time predictions concerning the duration of Israel's bondage to Antiochus. In Daniel 7, the question "How long?" is not asked *expressis verbis*, but is nonetheless assumed (cf. 7:25 and 12:6–7).

These visions lament the continuation of Antiochus' rule because it represents the final stage of Israel's "exile." This is indicated in Daniel 9, where both lament and time prediction are most fully developed.[2] The immediate concern in this chapter is the duration of the exile (v. 2), and it is this question which prompts Daniel's long penitential prayer (vss. 4–19) and secures the divine answer that Israel's exile is to be extended from seventy years to a period of seventy weeks of years, culminating in Antiochus' $3\frac{1}{2}$ years' oppression of Israel and his final destruction. With its promise of imminent deliverance from "exile," Daniel 9 indicates the perspective of the remaining visions, as can be seen from the following points of comparison:

a. *Reviews of history*. Just as Israelite history in Dan 9:24f. focuses on the period from the exile and return to the destruction of Antiochus, so the historical reviews of chapters 7–8, 10–12 are confined to the same period.

b. *Antiochus and the end of the "exile."* Dan 9:27 places the period of Antiochus' persecution at the latter half of the seventieth week, i.e., at the end of Israel's "exile." Similarly, the demise of Antiochus after $3\frac{1}{2}$ years in Dan 7:25 marks the end of an era extending from Babylon to Antiochus, since the judgment of the little horn precipitates the judgment of all four beasts (vss. 11–12). Daniel 8 shares the same perspective. Here the 2300-day persecution era occurs at "the latter end of the indignation (z^cm)" (v. 19) or "exile" (cf. z^cm Zech 1:12).[3] Again, in Dan 11:36, Antiochus' programme against Israel continues until the end of the "indignation" or "exilic" era.

c. *The "exile" a time of sin*. In Dan 9:24, the passing of 490 years brings to an end a period of transgression and sin. Similarly, in 8:23, Antiochus appears against Israel "when transgressors have reached their full measure." In both passages, the post-exilic period in its entirety is characterized as a period of sin.[4]

d. *Negative assessment of the nations of the "exile."* Dan 9:25 refers to the restoration programme during the 62 weeks as a "troubled time." Similarly, the parallelism[5] afforded by 8:23 ("the latter end of their [gentile] rule") and 8:19 ("the latter end of the [divine] indignation") indicates a negative assessment of gentile rule in the post-exilic era. Again, in Daniel

[2] Cf. Zimmerli 1976, 585.
[3] Cf. Plöger 1965, 128.
[4] Cf. Steck 1980, 66.
[5] Cf. Plöger 1965, 128.

10–12, Persia, Greece and Antiochus alike are regarded as enemies of Israel's heavenly army (10:20 cf. 11:40–12:1). In Daniel 7, all four kings are depicted as fighting beasts deserving judgment, while in chapter 8, aggressiveness and hubris characterize ram, he-goat and little horn alike.

The picture we have drawn of the exile in Daniel 7–12 is consistent with the viewpoint reflected in the intertestamental literature. Despite individual differences in presentation, these writings repeatedly view the exile as a period extending from the sixth century to a future divine intervention at the end-time.[6] Numerous laments and historical reviews from the intertestamental period give expression to this point of view,[7] and it is within the broader context of this stream of tradition that the lament formulae and eschatological visions of Daniel 7–12 are most readily explained.[8]

Lament imagery and the animal visions of Daniel 7 and 8

That OT laments (proto-apocalyptic, prophetic, psalmodic) from the exilic/post-exilic era inform the animal imagery of Daniel 7 and 8 is suggested by the following considerations:

a. *Proto-apocalyptic*. The visions of Daniel 7 and 8 are anticipated by the vision of Zech 2:1–4, in which horns or horned beasts (see below) representing Israel's exilic oppressors are subjected to divine punishment. This vision occurs in response to a lament concerning the delay of the nation's return from exile (1:12).

b. *Prophecy*. Daniel's dependence on Third Isaiah has been established by Nickelsburg,[9] and it is probable that reference in chapter 8 to (Michael) the "Prince" (v. 11), "truth" (v. 12) and the "sanctuary" (vss. 11, 13, 14) as targets of the little horn's attacks has been influenced by the exilic/post-exilic communal laments Isa 59:1–15a and 63:7–64:11. Both laments, which were probably used by visionary circles dissatisfied with the Zadokite restoration programme,[9a] feature pastoral imagery comparable to that of Daniel 8 (see below).

c. *Psalmody*. In several individual psalms of lament (e.g., Psalms 7, 10, 17, 22, 35, 59), the petitioner calls on God to judge his oppressors, who are depicted as predators or horned beasts. As Becker has argued, individual complaints of this sort probably received a collective, eschatological reinterpretation during the exilic/post-exilic period, whereby the foes of the individual came to symbolize Israel's gentile overlords who were to be

---

[6] See Knibb 1976, 253–272.
[7] See Gowan 1977, 205–223.
[8] Cf. Steck 1967, 155 n. 10.
[9] Nickelsburg 1972, 20–23.
[9a] See Hanson 1975, 79–100, 113–133.

judged at the end-time.[10] Certain collective psalms of lament presumably in use during the same period also call for divine judgment on the gentile nations, who are likewise represented as wild beasts (e.g., Psalms 58 and 74). Both individual and collective complaints from the book of Psalms consequently provide important parallels to Daniel 7, where God the judge secures eschatological deliverance from Israel's exilic/post-exilic gentile overlords, who are depicted as three predators and a horned beast.[11]

A. Proto-apocalyptic sources

Turning first of all to the vision of Zech 2:1–4, some preliminary considerations concerning the relation of Zechariah 1–8 to the book of Daniel are in order. Hanson has sought to contrast these chapters with Zechariah 9–14: whereas the former work simply uses apocalyptic motifs to legitimate a pragmatic political programme, only the latter is supposed to contain a genuine apocalyptic eschatology.[12] Such a contrast, however, fails to do justice to the significance of Zechariah 1–8 in the development of apocalyptic. As Mason has recently argued, "a real line of continuing tradition runs from proto- to deutero-Zechariah, in something of the same way that it is believed that Second Isaiah comes from within a continuing circle of Isaianic tradition."[13] Moreover, *an* eschatological element in Zechariah 1–8

---

[10] Becker finds specific traces of this development in Psalms 102, 69, 22, 107, 118, 66, 85, 59, 9–10, 56, 54, 108 and 68 (1966, 41–68). Numerous other laments doubtless received a similar eschatological orientation. In the LXX, over one third of the Psalms carry the superscription Εἰς τὸ τέλος.

[11] Cf. also Childs 1979, 517–518: " ... *one of the striking features of the Psalter in its canonical form is the large number of psalms which sound dominant eschatological notes* .... Many of these psalms exhibit all the stereotyped characteristics of the individual complaint psalms so carefully analysed by Gunkel. The psalmist fluctuates between complaints in his present plight, pleas for help, and outbursts of confidence in God. Although it is true that many psalms in this category end on the same note of complaint with which the psalm began (cf. Ps. 88, etc.), in many of these psalms the psalmist comforts himself, not by reflecting on events in the past, but by his hope in some future action of God which will be different in kind from that of the past .... However one explains it, *the final form of the Psalter is highly eschatological in nature. It looks toward the future and passionately yearns for its arrival.* Even when the psalmist turns briefly to reflect on the past in praise of the 'great things which Yahweh has done', invariably the movement shifts and again the hope of salvation is projected into the future (Ps. 126.6). *The perspective of Israel's worship in the Psalter is eschatologically oriented. As a result, the Psalter in its canonical form, far from being different in kind from the prophetic message, joins with the prophets in announcing God's coming kingship. When the New Testament heard in the psalms eschatological notes, its writers were standing in the context of the Jewish canon in which the community of faith worshipped and waited*" (italics ours).

[12] Hanson 1975, 250–253; 1976, 983.

[13] Mason 1976, 238.

cannot be denied,[14] and Jeremias has successfully demonstrated that the night visions occupy a transitional position between prophecy and apocalyptic, as represented by the book of Daniel.[15]

The vision of the horns

Zech 2:1–4 reads as follows:

And I lifted my eyes and saw, and behold, four horns! And I said to the angel who talked with me, What are these? And he answered me, These are the horns which have scattered Judah, Israel, and Jerusalem. Then the Lord showed me four smiths. And I said, What are these coming to do? He answered, These are the horns which scattered Judah, so that no man raised his head; and these have come to terrify them, to cast down the horns of the nations who lifted up their horns against the land of Judah to scatter it.

This vision, which dates from the year 522/1 (cf. 1:7), develops the previous vision's theme of Yahweh's wrath against Judah's gentile oppressors (cf. 1:14).[16] The promise of divine intervention introduced in 1:14f. in turn comes in response to an angelic lament concerning the duration of the exile (1:12):

Then the angel of the Lord said, O Lord of hosts, how long wilt thou have no mercy on Jerusalem and the cities of Judah, against which thou hast had indignation these seventy years?

The vision of the horns consequently occurs in a context which includes (1) reference to the angelic intermediary (Zech 1:12 cf. Dan 8:13; 12:6); (2) the lament formula "How long?" (Zech 1:12 cf. Dan 8:13; 12:6); (3) reference to the "indignation" (Zech 1:12 cf. Dan 8:19; 11:36), (4) the seventy years (Zech 1:12 cf. Dan 9:2, 24) and (5) the divine answer (Zech 1:13 cf. Dan 8:14; 12:7). Since this cluster of motifs is strikingly reproduced in the visions of Daniel, it is highly probable that the vision of the horns itself anticipates the animal visions of Daniel 7 and 8, in which horn symbolism is a prominent feature.

More specifically, the vision of the horns may be compared with the animal visions of Daniel in the following ways:[17]

a. In both Zechariah and Daniel, horns symbolize enemy powers (Zech 2:4; Dan 7:24–25; 8:23f.).

b. In both works, horns represent beasts. In Zech 2:4, *ḥrd* hi. ("to

---

[14] Cf. Knibb 1982, 175.

[15] See C. Jeremias 1977, 88–108.

[16] Cf. C. Jeremias 1977, 24, 156.

[17] For some of the following comparisons between Zechariah and Daniel, see already C. Jeremias 1977, 156–163.

terrify") most naturally refers to the beasts carrying the horns.[18] Similarly, the great words of the little horn in Daniel 7 precipitate the destruction of the beast which carries it (Dan 7:11, 12),[19] while the little horn of chapter 8 assumes the characteristics of the he-goat by casting its victims to the ground and trampling upon them (vss. 10–13 cf. v. 7).[20]

c. Whereas the horns in Zechariah 2 scatter Judah (v. 4), the little horn of Dan 7:21 makes war on the saints (cf. also Dan 8:24).

d. The horns of Zechariah 2, which are four in number, are suggestive of the four beasts of Daniel 7, the fourth of which is horned.[21] Although Zechariah 2 makes no mention of consecutive powers as in Daniel 7, traces of contemporaneity in Daniel 7 are suggested by the four winds or compass points, which presumably correspond to the four beasts emerging from the sea (Dan 7:2, 3).[22]

e. Just as the horns of the nations are "cast down" by divine intervention in Zech 2:4, so the horned beast of Daniel 7 is destroyed in the judgment (7:11), while Antiochus, the little horn of the vision of chapter 8, is "broken" by divine intervention (8:25).

f. The agents accomplishing the punishment of the four horns or beasts of Zechariah 2 are referred to as "smiths" (ḥršym). Such are comparable to the ʾnšym bʿrym ḥršy mšḥyt of Eze 21:36, who are similarly called to punish a power opposed to Israel.[23] Since these warrior smiths destroy Yahweh's enemies with refiner's fire (Eze 21:36–37 cf. 22:21, 31), it is possible that in Zechariah 2, the four smiths threaten the four horns or beasts with a similar fate.[24] In this regard, it is perhaps significant that in Daniel 7, the ten-horned beast is also destroyed by fire in the judgment (vss. 10–11). Such being the case, both Zechariah and Daniel might be said to depict the "exile" as a

---

[18] C. Jeremias, who observes that ḥrd hi. is used in relation to animals in Deut 28:26; Jer 7:33 (birds), Isa 17:2 (flocks) and Nah 2:12 (lions), notes the possibility "dass in dieser Formulierung von Sach 2, 4 der Lebensbereich durchscheint, in dem die übertragene Redeweise vom Horn als Symbol der Stärke ihren Ursprung hat: Die Hörner tragenden Tiere werden aufgeschreckt" (1977, 159).

[19] Cf. Behrmann 1894, 47.

[20] For a comparable instance of synecdoche, see Testament of Joseph 19, in which three stags or three lambs in v. 3 are referred to in v. 9 as "three horns." The rationale for some of these cases of *pars pro toto* possibly lies in the representative role of the ruler, whose person stands for the people over which he is placed. Cf. Dan 8:20–22, where horns stand for both kings and kingdoms.

[21] Cf. von Rad 1965, 2:312 n. 25.

[22] Cf. Ginsberg 1948, 70 n. 36.

[23] Cf. C. Jeremias 1977, 160–161.

[24] Cf. the "refinement" inflicted on Israel the flock in Zech 13:9. In Ezekiel 21–22, however, the fire of the refiner effects total destruction.

period of bondage to various beasts, whose supremacy is terminated by divine intervention with fire.

We shall now examine the rationale underlying the horn imagery in Zech 2:1–4. There is reason to believe that both the gentile nations and Judah are depicted as horned beasts in these verses. This is indicated by the twofold appearance of the verb *nś'* in v. 4: just as the gentile nations lift up (*nś'*) their horns in order to scatter Judah, so the scattered inhabitants of Judah are unable to raise (*nś'*) their heads.[25] In both instances, *nś'* suggests the mode in which the ox uses its horns, viz., lowering the head and then tossing it up (cf. Ps 92:10–11).[26] Consistent with this interpretation is the use of *zrh* pi. ("scatter") in 2:4, which is used of Israel the warrior flock in Ps 44:12. Zech 2:4, therefore, probably calls to mind the picture of Judah as a herd of cattle who are scattered and oppressed by the horned beasts of the gentile nations. Bearing in mind that several traditions in Zechariah 1–8 reappear in deutero-Zechariah,[27] we suggest that the rationale for the horn imagery in Zech 2:1–4 is developed in Zechariah 10 and 11, which depict Israel the flock under captivity to her foreign overlords or shepherds. The following passages invite comparison:

a. Divine anger against the gentile rulers or nations:

Zech 1:15	*Zech 10:3*
And I am very angry with the nations that are at ease ...	My anger is hot against the shepherds ...

That the "shepherds" in Zech 10:3 are gentile overlords rather than Israelite rulers is indicated by mention of the flock's ingathering from exile in vss. 4–12, as well as reference to the "sceptre" of Egypt in v. 11, which is probably an allusion to the shepherd's staff as a symbol of royalty.[28]

b. Gentile overlords depicted as horns or horned beasts:

Zech 2:4	*Zech 10:3*
the horns of the nations who lifted up their horns against the land of Judah to scatter it.	and I will punish the "he-goats" (*'twdym*) ...

---

[25] The antiquity of the metaphor and its pastoralist origins are suggested by the following lines occurring in a neo-Sumerian hymn to Enlil, shepherd god and founder of Nippur (lines 71–72): "Like a steer, it raises up its horns in Sumer, All the lands bow their heads" (Reisman 1969, 62).

[26] Cf. Houghton 1863, 1595–1596.

[27] See Mason 1976, 227–239. (Cf. n. 13 above).

[28] Vancil 1975, 241–242.

c. Gentile overlords depicted as warriors:

Zech 2:4

These are the horns which
scattered Judah, so that no man
raised his head ...

Zech 11:5–6

Those who buy them slay them and
go unpunished; and those who *sell*
them say, Blessed be the Lord,
I have become rich; and their
own shepherds have no pity on
them.
For I will no longer have
pity on the inhabitants of this
land, says the Lord. Lo, I will
cause men to fall each *into the
hand* of his shepherd, and each
into the hand of his king; and
they shall crush the earth, and
I will deliver none from their
hand.

The cruel shepherds[29] of 11:6 are the buyers of 11:5, who are to be identified as enemies of Israel. This is evident from the use made in these verses of the expression "to sell into the hand," which belongs to the terminology of holy war (cf. Jud 3:8; 4:2, 9; 10:7–8; 1 Sam 12:9; Ps 44:13). Already in the Sumerian *Song to Enlil*, Enlil the shepherd is addressed as both a wild bull which none can frighten (cf. Zech 2:4) and as a merchant (cf. Zech 11:5–6):

Father Mullil, shepherd of the "black-headed,"

Father Mullil, wild bull, who leads the men,
Father Mullil, who sleeps a light sleep,
reclining wild bull, bull, whom no one frightens,
Mullil, merchant of the wide earth,
Lord, whose consort is the trader of the earth.[30]

d. Armies of Judah depicted as a scattered flock or herd:

Zech 2:4

the horns which scattered Judah,
so that no man raised his head ...
the nations who lifted up their
horns against the land of Judah
to scatter it.

Zech 10:3, 9

the Lord of hosts cares for his
flock, the house of Judah, and
will make them like his proud
steed in battle ...
Though I scattered them among
the nations, yet in far
countries they shall remember me ...

As we shall now argue below, the apparent identification of kings and warriors with both horned beasts and shepherds in proto- and deutero-

---

[29] Reading *rō ᶜēhû* instead of *rᶜēhû*.
[30] Falkenstein 1953, 76 (lines 5, 7–11).

Zechariah is to be explained in the light of the following external metaphors: (1) The herd leader is the SHEPHERD of the flock; (2) The military leader is the SHEPHERD of the warriors; (3) The warrior is the (destructive) SHEPHERD of the enemy; (4) The ruler is the SHEPHERD of the nation.

(1) The herd leader is the SHEPHERD of the flock

In Zech 10:3, shepherds are mentioned in parallelism with he-goats:

My anger is hot against the shepherds, and I will punish the "he-goats" (*ᶜtwdym*); for the Lord of hosts cares for his flock, the house of Judah, and will make them like his proud steed in battle.

This association of ideas is most readily explained in the light of the Near Eastern notion of the herd leader, which from earliest times symbolized the office of shepherd kings and shepherd gods.

a. *Mesopotamian herd leaders.* Numerous Mesopotamian texts refer to either the shepherd king or the shepherd god as an ox, bull, wild cow or bellwether, thus indicating that "herd leader" as a royal or divine title was synonymous with "shepherd":

Father Mullil, shepherd of the "black-headed,"

Father Mullil, wild bull, who leads the men,
Father Mullil, who sleeps a light sleep,
reclining wild bull, bull whom no one frightens[31]

a wild bull who goes ahead, whom no one opposes,
a wild bull with bright eyes shining,

Lipitishtar, the king of the land of Sumer am I,
the good shepherd of the "black-headed"[32]

Primeval bull, just shepherd of An[33]

The noble wild cow of Enlil am I,
his noble wild cow who goes ahead of all.[34]

Compare:

Thy (gracious) "sufficient!" O Ruler of heaven and earth,
Thou shepherdess of the *clouded* people[35]

Thou, Mullil, ... the shepherd of the black-headed!
Thou wild bull, who leads the hosts, thou, the ruler,
the godly wild bull of the upper and lower world.[36]

---

[31] Falkenstein 1953, 76 (lines 5, 7–9).
[32] Falkenstein 1953, 126 (lines 9–10, 17–18).
[33] Nagel 1964, 226 n. 108.
[34] Falkenstein 1953, 68 (lines 13–14).
[35] Falkenstein 1953, 329 (line 27).
[36] Witzel 1935, 169 (Nr. 13).

The great mountain, father Enlil, lies down dreaming.
The shepherd of the black-headed lies down dreaming.
He who witnesses everything himself lies down dreaming.
The bull who causes the troops to wander lies down dreaming.

The ox residing in the cattle pen lies down dreaming.
The sheep residing in the sheepfold lies down dreaming.[37]

Enlil, the bull who is sleeping, why does he not rise?
The bison, the bull who is sleeping, why does he not rise?
Father Enlil, why does he not rise?
The bison, why does he not rise?

The goring bull, why does he not rise?[38]

I praise the ox, the great steer, Umungirra.
I praise the ox, the lord who leads the cattle.

The goring steer, father Enlil, has made you lofty,
The handsome steer, father Enlil, has made you lofty.[39]

As Seibert has argued, it is possible that the herd leader title for the shepherd preserves the memory of the taming of wild flocks and herds, whereby the human shepherd assumed the position of the animal leader:

... mit der Zähmung und Beherrschung der einst wildlebenden Herde war der Mensch seit einer langen Reihe von Jahrhunderten zum Leiter, zum Führer der Herden geworden, hatte gewissermassen die Stelle des Leittieres eingenommen. Als Führer der Menschen wird nun der König dementsprechend zum Leittier der Menschenherde! Der "vorangehende Wildstier", der die Mannen "anführt", ist also gleich Hirt bzw. König zu setzen .... Noch im 1. Jt. v. u. Z. finden sich Beispiele für die Bezeichnung des Königs als Leittier: Sanherib und Nabonid werden als kluger bzw. hervorragender "Leithammel" tituliert. Diese Gleichsetzung des "vorangehenden Wildstieres" mit dem "Hirten" weist gleichzeitig sinnfällig auf eine entwicklungsgeschichtliche Abfolge hin, die für uns im einzelnen zwar nicht rekonstruierbar ist, aber doch so verlaufen sein muss, dass dem Menschen die wildlebende Herde, die er verfolgte und belauerte, beherrschte und zähmte, eines Tages untertan war. Er, nunmehr ihr "Leittier" und "Hirt", hat vermutlich in einem ähnlich komplizierten und langdauernden Unterwerfungs- und Entwicklungsprozess sich auch die Menschenherde untertan gemacht, wurde auch ihr Hirt, ihr König, und bezeichnete sich ebenfalls als ihr "Leittier". Diese Attribute des Königs: Leittier, vorangehender Stier u. ä., dürften also ebenfalls dem Hirtenleben entlehnt worden sein.[40]

b. *OT herd leaders.* In view of the Mesopotamian evidence identifying shepherds with herd leaders, it is probable that the following OT references

---

[37] Cohen 1972, 337 (lines 23'–24', 27'–28').
[38] Cohen 1972, 288 (lines 22–25, 17').
[39] Cohen 1972, 135–136 (lines 42–43, 71–72).
[40] Seibert 1969, 13–14.

to shepherds used in parallelism or association with he-goats, rams or bulls should be treated as further instances of the same metaphor:

he-goats

In addition to Zech 10:3 (see above), he-goats represent shepherds in Isa 14:9 and Eze 34:17:

Isa 14:9

Sheol beneath is stirred up to meet you when you come, it rouses the shades to greet you, all who were "he-goats" (ᶜ*twdy*) of the earth; it raises from their thrones all who were kings of the nations.

Here the king of Babylon joins the ᶜ*twdym* or kings of the nations in the underworld. Reference to his broken staff in Isa 14:5 indicates that the king of Babylon is a shepherd king (cf. Isa 14:29–30; Zech 11:7, 10, 14).

Eze 34:17

As for you, my flock, thus says the Lord God: Behold, I judge between sheep and sheep, rams and he-goats (ᶜ*twdym*).

The rams and he-goats of Eze 34:17f. are to be identified with the shepherds of vss. 2–16. This is suggested by the parallel concerns of both sections of the chapter. The first section (vss. 2–16) accuses the shepherds of Israel of feeding themselves (vss. 2, 8, 10), neglecting the flock (vss. 2, 3, 4, 8), and ruling with force and harshness (v. 4), so that the sheep are scattered (vss. 5, 6, 12) and become a prey to wild beasts (vss. 5, 8, 10). Consequently, God will rescue his sheep from the shepherds and the nations (vss. 10–12), and feed them on the mountains of Israel with justice (vss. 13–16). Similarly, in the second section (vss. 17ff.), the rams and he-goats are depicted as feeding on good pasture (v. 18), depriving the flock of their natural rights (v. 19), pushing and thrusting at the weak (v. 21), so that the sheep are scattered abroad (v. 21) and become a prey (v. 22). Consequently, God will save his flock (v. 22), judge between sheep and sheep (vss. 20, 22), and feed them on his holy hill (vss. 26, 29). In view of these parallel concerns underlying both vss. 2–16 and vss. 17–31, the oppressive members of the flock in the latter half of the chapter should be identified with the shepherds mentioned already in the first section.

This conclusion is supported by the MT of v. 16, which reads "and the fat and the strong I will destroy (ʾ*šmyd*). If the MT offers the correct reading, then mention is already made here, in the first section of the chapter, of judgment to be meted out on the fat sheep, as in vss. 17ff. V. 16, moreover, refers directly back to v. 4: what the faithless shepherds have *failed* to do (v. 4), God, the owner of the sheep, himself promises to accomplish (v. 16).

(Most of v. 4 is presented in reverse order in v. 16, although reference to the sick in v. 4 finds no direct counterpart in the latter verse):

Eze 34:4

The weak you have not strengthened, the sick you have not healed, the crippled you have not bound up, the strayed you have not brought back, the lost you have not sought, and with force (*hzqh*) and harshness you have ruled them.

Eze 34:16

I will seek the lost, and I will bring back the strayed, and I will bind up the crippled, and I will strengthen the weak, and the fat and the strong (*hzqh*) I will destroy.

Of interest here is that *hzqh* ("force") in v. 4 corresponds to *hhzqh* ("the strong") in v. 16. The fat and strong sheep who are destroyed in v. 16, therefore, are the oppressive shepherds who rule the flock with force and harshness in v. 4. Since it is the same fat sheep who thrust at the weak with their horns in v. 21, they are to be identified with the shepherds or rulers of Israel.

rams

As noted above, rams represent shepherds in Ezekiel 34. A similar association of ideas occurs in Jer 32:34 LXX:

Howl, ye shepherds, and cry; and lament, ye rams of the flock: for your days have been completed for slaughter, and ye shall fall as the choice rams.

In Eze 31:14, rams are used in parallelism with trees:

All this in order that no trees by the waters may grow to lofty height or set their tops among the clouds, and that no "rams" (*'lyhm*) that drink water may reach up to them in height ...

This passage is of interest, since the tree is a shepherd symbol both in the OT and in Mesopotamia (see below).

bulls

Bulls are referred to as shepherds in Gen 49:24, 1 Sam 21:8 and 1 Kings 22:11, 17:

Gen 49:24–25

Yet his bow remained unmoved, his arms were made agile by the hands of the *'byr* of Jacob (by the name of the Shepherd, the Rock of Israel), by the God of your father who will help you, by God Almighty who will bless you ...

Comparison with Ugaritic texts suggests that "Bull" is the preferred rendering of *'byr* in v. 24:

Gen 49:24–25 is particularly interesting because in these lines—heavy with Canaanite influence—the appellative "Bull of Jacob" appears in close relationship to

72

ʾēl-ʾābîkā, which Vawter ... translates as "El thy Father," noting the Ugaritic expression *il ab*, which appears in various combinations and with pronominal suffixes. It most frequently appears in combination with *ṯr* "bull" as in UT 49: IV: 34, *ṯr il abk*, "Bull El, thy Father." In this very early poem the author seems to be drawing upon traditional El terminology in describing Yahweh (cf. El Shaddai in vs. 25).[41]

1 Sam 21:8

Now a certain man of the servants of Saul was there that day, detained before the Lord; his name was Doeg the Edomite, the ʾ*byr* of Saul's *rᶜym*.

As Miller has noted,[42] ʾ*byr* in this verse is an animal designation for a leader. Comparable is Ps 68:31, which speaks of rebuking "the assembly/herd of bulls (ᶜ*dt* ʾ*byrym*) with the calves (ᶜ*gly*) of the peoples." Here it would appear that bulls and calves are nobles or princes.

1 Kings 22:11, 17

And Zedekiah the son of Chenaanah made for himself horns of iron, and said, Thus says the Lord, With these you shall push the Syrians until they are destroyed.

And he [Micaiah] said, I saw all Israel scattered upon the mountains, as sheep that have no shepherd; and the Lord said, These have no master; let each return to his home in peace.

Zedekiah's oracle to Ahab is reminiscent of Deut 33:17, where the tribe of Joseph is associated with a bull or wild ox:

His firstling bull has majesty, and his horns are the horns of a wild ox; with them he shall push the peoples, all of them, to the ends of the earth; ...

Micaiah, on the other hand, speaks of Ahab as shepherd of the armies of Israel. Since both prophets employ horned-beast imagery to describe either the king or his warriors, it is probable that the iron horns of 1 Kings 22:11 represent Ahab as herd leader or shepherd.

    c. *Apocalyptic herd leaders*. Apocalyptic passages describing herd leaders are 1 Enoch 89–90, Testament of Joseph 19 and Daniel 7–8.

1 Enoch 89–90

In the Animal Apocalypse, herd leaders represent kings or warriors in charge of Israel the flock. Our review of Mesopotamian and OT instances of the herd-leader idea would suggest that the rams leading the flock in the following passages should also be regarded as shepherds (1 En 89:42–43, 45–47, 49; 90:9–10, 12, 16, 19):

And the dogs and the foxes and the wild-boars began to devour those sheep until the Lord of the sheep raised up a ram from among them which led them. And that ram

---

[41] Miller 1967, 421 n. 36.
[42] Miller 1971, 180.

began to butt those dogs and foxes and wild-boars, on one side and on the other, until it had destroyed them all.

And the Lord of the sheep sent the sheep to another sheep and raised it up to be a ram, and to lead the sheep in place of that sheep which had renounced its glory. And it went to it, and spoke with it alone, and raised up that ram, and made it the prince and leader of the sheep; and during all this those dogs oppressed the sheep. And the first ram pursued that second ram, and that second ram rose and fled before it.

And those sheep grew and increased; but all the dogs and foxes and wild-boars were afraid and fled from it, and that ram butted and killed all the animals, and those animals did not again prevail amongst the sheep and did not seize anything further from them.

And I looked until horns came up on these lambs, but the ravens cast their horns down; and I looked until a big horn grew on one of those sheep, and their eyes were opened. And it looked at them, and their eyes were opened, and it cried to the sheep, and the rams saw it, and they all ran to it.

And those ravens battled and fought with it, and wished to make away with its horn, but they did not prevail against it.

All the eagles and vultures and ravens and kites gathered together and brought with them all the wild sheep, and they all came together and helped one another in order to dash that horn of the ram in pieces.

And I looked until a big sword was given to the sheep, and the sheep went out against all the wild animals to kill them, and all the animals and the birds of heaven fled before them.

Testament of Joseph 19

In Test Jos 19:6–9, the fourth bull and the lamb which protect the flocks are comparable to herd leaders in the Animal Apocalypse, and are thus appropriate symbols of the messianic shepherd figure depicted in these verses:

And the horns of the fourth bull were elevated up to the heavens and became like a wall for the flocks and another horn flowered between the horns. And I saw a calf which circled it twelve times and became an aid to the bulls altogether. And I saw among the horns a virgin who had a many-coloured garment and from her a lamb went forth. And from its right side all wild beasts and creeping things attacked and the lamb overcame them and destroyed them. And the bulls and the cow and the three horns were glad because of it and rejoiced with it.

Daniel 7–8

In spite of their anomalous physical characteristics (see Chapter Two), the ten-horned beast, the ram and the he-goat of Daniel 7 and 8 are to be identified as herd leaders or shepherds:

The ten-horned beast

Comparable to the multiple horns of the ten-horned beast are the multiple-horned crowns associated with gods and monsters in Mesopotamian art:

It is stated that the fourth beast has ten horns, just as in the plastic arts of Mesopo-

74

tamia many gods in human form—and also many daemonic monsters—wore a crown of horns with several pairs of bull's horns arranged one above the other.[43]

Here one thinks of the man-headed oxen unearthed at Lagash and dating from the time of Gudea,[44] or the considerably later *lamassu* which guarded the entrances of Assyrian palaces.[45] As Jastrow argued early this century, monstrosities of this sort in Mesopotamian art testify to the widespread influence of birth divination notions in the ancient world.[46] It will be shown below that already in the neo-Sumerian period, the shepherd king depicted himself as a birth anomaly, and Seibert is surely correct when she identifies the multiple-horned crown with Mesopotamian shepherd gods and shepherd kings in their capacity as herd leaders:

In dem Zusammenhang Leittier gleich König muss auch das Vorkommen der Hörnerkrone, die von göttlichen Wesen und vergöttlichten Königen getragen wird, in der altorientalischen Bildkunst gesehen werden. Es scheint mir naheliegend, dass die Gedankengänge und Vorstellungen, die den altorientalischen Menschen veranlassten, seine Herrscher und Götter gleicherweise "führender Wildstier" und "Hirt" zu nennen, ihn mit dazu brachten, dies auch bildmässig durch die Kombination Mensch plus Hörnerkrone zum Ausdruck zu bringen. Die Darstellungen von Stieren mit menschlichem Gesicht und mehrfacher Hörnerkrone lassen den Gedanken an eine derartige Kombination ebenfalls aufkommen, ebenso die Tatsache, dass manche Stiere kostbare Königsbärte tragen. Mit der Textstelle aus einer Hymne Lipitischtars wird diese Verbindung König–Stier–Königsbart treffend illustriert: "bin ein Wildstier, der vorangeht, ein Wisenstier, leuchtend mit buntem Auge, trage einen langen Bart wie aus Lapislazuli."[47]

Mention in Dan 7:8 of "another horn" emerging amongst the ten furnishes further support for the view that the ten-horned beast is a herd leader. In Chapter Two, we compared this verse with Test Jos 19:6, where "another horn" appears between the horns of the fourth bull (Judah):

Dan 7:8	*Test Jos 19:6*
I considered the horns, and behold, there came up among them another horn, a little one ...	And the horns of the fourth bull were elevated up to the heavens and became like a wall for the flocks and another horn flowered between the horns.

In Test Jos 19:6, however, reference to the bull's horns as a "wall for the flocks" indicates the animal's role as shepherd. The expression is reminis-

[43] Noth 1966, 212.
[44] Parrot 1962, 224 (figs. 276–277).
[45] See Buttrick (ed.) 1962, 4:224 (fig. 29).
[46] Jastrow 1914, 60–61, 63.
[47] Seibert 1969, 14.

cent of 1 Sam 25:16, where the men protecting Nabal's shepherds are referred to as a "wall":

they were a wall to us both by night and by day, all the while we were with them keeping the sheep.[48]

The ram

A key verb used in connection with the ram is *ngh* pi. in Dan 8:4:

I saw the ram charging (*mngh*) westward and northward and southward;
no beast could stand before him, and there was no one who could rescue from his power; he did as he pleased and magnified himself.

Elsewhere in the OT, *ngh* pi., when used in connection with horned-beast symbolism, consistently describes the action of herd-leaders or shepherds. (See Deut 33:17—Joseph (cf. Gen 49:22—Joseph *bn prt* "son of cow"[49] and Gen 49:24—Joseph's heavenly counterpart is shepherd-bull); 1 Kings 22:11=2 Chron 18:10—Ahab (cf. 1 Kings 22:17=2 Chron 18:16—Ahab the shepherd of Israel's armies); Ps 44:6—God (cf. vss. 12, 23, and v. 24 cf. Nah 3:18—God the shepherd of Israel's armies); Eze 34:21 cf. vss 4–6—shepherds of Israel).

Again, as noted in Chapter Four, Dan 8:4 LXX has κερατίξοντα for *ngh* pi. In 1 En 89:42–43 Vat., however, κερατίξειν describes the action of a herd-leader ram:

And the dogs and the foxes and the wild-boars began to devour those sheep until the Lord of the sheep raised up a ram from among them which led them. And that ram began to butt (Vat. κερατίξειν) those dogs and foxes and wild-boars, on one side and on the other, until it had destroyed them all.

The he-goat

The vision of the he-goat, whose little horn attacks the Jerusalem cult "at the latter end of the indignation" (Dan 8:19), belongs to the OT tradition of the eschatological enemy from the north. Such is indicated by the following considerations:

(1) Mention in Dan 8:23 of Antiochus as "a king of bold countenance" alludes to Deut 28:49, 50: "a nation ... from afar ... a nation of stern countenance"—a concept closely akin to the enemy from the north tradition (cf. references to an enemy "from a distant land," "from afar," etc. in Jer 4:16; 5:15; 6:22; Isa 5:26; 10:3; 13:5; 30:27; 39:3; Hab 1:8).

---

[48] In the Revelation of John, Daniel 7's ten-horned beast (13:1–2) becomes the adversary and opposite number of the seven-horned Lamb, who is depicted in 7:17 as shepherd of the great multitude, and in 14:1–5 as herd leader of the twelve tribes. The latter are depicted as "spotless" sacrificial sheep (14:5 cf. 1 Pet 1:19) in whose mouth no lie is found (14:5 cf. Isa 53:7, 9; Zeph 3:13), and who follow the Lamb wherever he goes (14:4).
[49] For this reading see Salo 1968, 94–95.

(2) Dan 11:40–45 describes Antiochus' eschatological assault in terms of traditions already brought together in Eze 39:1–5, namely, the enemy from the north (cf. Jeremiah 1–6) and the enemy slain on the mountains of Israel or in the vicinity of Jerusalem (Isa 14:24–25; 31:8–9).[50]

(3) In Eze 39:17–20, however, the slain enemy from the north (cf. vss. 1–5) are depicted as fighting horned beasts representing princes and warriors:[51]

As for you, son of man, thus says the Lord God: Speak to the birds of every sort and to all beasts of the field, Assemble and come, gather from all sides to the sacrificial feast which I am preparing for you, a great sacrificial feast upon the mountains of Israel, ... You shall eat the flesh of the mighty, and drink the blood of *the princes of the earth—of rams, of lambs, and of goats, of bulls*, all of them fatlings of Bashan. And you shall eat fat till you are filled, and drink blood till you are drunk, at the sacrificial feast which I am preparing for you. And you shall be filled at my table with horses and riders, with *mighty men and all kinds of warriors*, says the Lord God.

Since Daniel 8 depicts Jerusalem's eschatological adversary as the horn of a fighting he-goat and as "a king of bold countenance" comparable to the "king of the north" of Dan 11:40–45, it is probable that the he-goat image in Daniel 8 partly derives from Ezekiel 39, in which he-goats and other horned beasts represent the latter-day enemy from the north. These fighting beasts, however, inevitably remind us of the enemy from the north in Jeremiah 6, who are depicted as warrior shepherds and warrior flocks (vss. 1–5):

Flee for safety, O people of Benjamin, from the midst of Jerusalem! Blow the trumpet in Tekoa, and raise a signal on Beth-hac-cherem; for *evil looms out of the north*, and great destruction. The comely and delicately bred I will destroy, the daughter of Zion. *Shepherds with their flocks shall come against her*; they shall pitch their tents around her, *they shall pasture, each in his place*. Prepare war against her; up, and let us attack at noon! Woe to us, for the day declines, for the shadows of evening lengthen! Up, and let us attack by night, and destroy her palaces!

In view of this, the horned beasts of Eze 39:18 and the he-goat of Daniel 8, which represent rulers and military leaders, are to be identified as herd leaders or shepherds.

The vision of the little horn in Dan 8:9–14 also expresses the OT theme that the instrument used to punish Israel frequently oversteps its permissible limits through hubris (cf. *gdl* Dan 8:11; Isa 10:15). Reference to the horn's attack against the heavenly host may therefore be compared with Isaiah's satirical poem against the arrogant king of Babylon in Isaiah 14:

---

[50] Cf. Erling 1972, 112.
[51] Cf. Miller 1971, 184: "The sacrificial image [in Isa 34:6–7; Eze 39:18] contributes to the rationale for designating certain classes or types by animal names but is not wholly determinative. The prophets prefer those animals which are not only sacrificial animals but are also used in other contexts metaphorically to designate leaders, dignitaries or warriors."

Isa 14:9, 10, 13, 14	*Dan 8:8, 10–11*
all who were "he-goats"	Then the he-goat (*ṣpyr hʿzym*)
(ʿ*twdy*) of the earth ...	magnified himself exceedingly ...
... will speak and say to	[its horn] grew great, even to
you ...	the host of heaven; and some of
You have become like us!	the stars it cast down to the
You said in your heart, I will	ground and trampled upon them.
ascend to heaven; above the	It magnified itself, even up to
stars of God I will set my	the Prince of the host.
throne on high ...	
I will ascend above the	
heights of the clouds, I will	
make myself like the Most High.	

As was noted above, the king of Babylon who joins the he-goats in Isaiah 14 is a shepherd king, (cf. Isa 14:5, 29–30; Zech 11:7, 10, 14), and the above comparison furnishes further support for the view that the he-goat of Daniel 8 is likewise to be regarded as a herd leader or shepherd.

Finally, it should be noted that the he-goat in Daniel is depicted in v. 5 as a unicorn, and that in Chapters Two and Four of our study, this verse was compared with 1 En 90:9, where a unicorn ram represents Judas Maccabaeus. The fact that this ram clearly functions as a leader of the other rams is consistent with our identification of the unicorned he-goat of Daniel 8 as a herd leader or shepherd.[52]

(2) The military leader is the SHEPHERD of the warriors

In Zechariah 10, Yahweh delivers his warrior flock from their gentile overlords or shepherds (vss. 3, 5, 8–11):

My anger is hot against the shepherds, and I will punish the "he-goats;" for the Lord of hosts cares for his flock, the house of Judah, and will make them like his proud steed in battle.

Together they shall be like mighty men in battle, trampling the foe in the mud of the streets; they shall fight because the Lord is with them, and they shall confound the riders on horses.

I will signal for them and gather them in, for I have redeemed them, and they shall be as many as of old. Though I scattered them among the nations, yet in far countries they shall remember me ... I will bring them home from the land of Egypt, and

---

[52] In March 1933, Dr. William F. Dove of the University of Maine created a unicorn bull by transplanting the animal's horn buds shortly after it was born. Possession of a single horn imparted to the bull the essential characteristics of a herd leader: "True in spirit as in horn to his prototype, he is conscious of peculiar power. Although he is an animal with hereditary potentiality for two horns, he recognizes the power of a single horn which he uses as a prow to pass under fences and barriers in his path, or as a forward thrusting bayonet in his attacks" (Dove 1936, 435).

gather them from Assyria; and I will bring them to the land of Gilead and to Lebanon, till there is no room for them. They shall pass through the sea of Egypt, and the waves of the sea shall be smitten, and all the depths of the Nile dried up. The pride of Assyria shall be laid low, and the scepter of Egypt shall depart.

Reference to warrior shepherds or warrior flocks occurs in the following texts (Mesopotamian, Greek, OT and apocalyptic), several of which also depict fighting herd leaders:

a. *Mesopotamian warrior shepherds*:

Thou Mullil, ... the *shepherd* of the black-headed,
Thou wild bull, who leads the hosts [53]

a wild bull who goes ahead, whom no one opposes,
a bison bull with bright eyes shining,

Lipitishtar, the king of the land of Sumer am I,
the good *shepherd* of the "black-headed",

the hero with the shining eyes, *who roars loudly (in battle),*
Lipitishtar, Enlil's son, am I. [54]

The slaughter he has given to me, the tumult he has given to me.

The gods are like (anxious) birds—but I am the Lady,
the Anunna gods run around startled—but I am the noble wild cow.
Enlil's noble wild cow am I,
his noble *wild cow who goes ahead of all.* [55]

When I stand before the slaughter, I am the *leading goat* of all lands. [56]

The shepherd of the black-headed lies down dreaming.

The *bull who causes the troops to wander* lies down dreaming. [57]

Hammurabi, *the shepherd*, called by Enlil, am I,

the fiery *wild bull who gores the foe* [58]

b. *Greek warrior shepherds*:

I grudge not that Agamemnon *shepherd of the host* should urge on the well-greaved Achaians to fight ...

But for the Trojans, like sheep beyond number that stand in the courtyard of a man of great substance, to be milked of their white milk, and bleat without ceasing to hear their lambs' cry, even so arose the clamour of the Trojans through the wide host. [59]

---

[53] Witzel 1935, 169 (Nr. 13).
[54] Falkenstein 1953, 126–129 (lines 9–10, 17–18, 78–79).
[55] Falkenstein 1953, 67–68 (lines 5, 11–14).
[56] Falkenstein 1944, 92.
[57] Cohen 1972, 337 (lines 23', 24').
[58] Pritchard (ed.) 1950, 164–165.
[59] Lang, Leaf and Myers n.d., 70–71 (Book IV).

So saying bright-eyed Athene went her way and Tydeides returned and entered the forefront of the battle; even though erst his soul was eager to do battle with the Trojans, yet now did threefold courage come upon him, as upon a lion whom some shepherd in the field guarding his fleecy sheep hath wounded, being sprung into the fold, yet hath not vanquished him; he hath roused his might, and then cannot beat him back, but lurketh amid the steading, and his forsaken flock is affrighted; so the sheep are cast in heaps, one upon the other, and the lion in his fury leapeth out of the high fold; even so in fury mingled mighty Diomedes with the Trojans. There slew he Astynoos and Hypeiron *shepherd of the host* ...[60]

And even as the *goatherds* easily divide the ranging flocks of goats when they mingle in the pasture, so did their *captains* marshal them on this side and on that, to enter into the fray, and in their midst lord Agamemnon, his head and eyes like unto Zeus whose joy is in the thunder, and his waist like unto Ares and his breast unto Poseidon. *Even as a bull standeth out far foremost amid the herd, for he is pre-eminent amid the pasturing kine, even such did Zeus make Atreides on that day, pre-eminent among many and chief amid heroes.*[61]

His armour lieth upon the bounteous earth, *and himself like a bell-wether rangeth the ranks of warriors.* Yea, I liken him to a thick-fleeced ram ordering a great flock of white ewes.[62]

and then the hosts followed them, as sheep follow their leader to the water from the pasture, and the shepherd is glad at heart; even so the heart of Aineias was glad in his breast, *when he saw the hosts of the people following to aid him.*[63]

c. *OT warrior shepherds*:

Gen 49:23–24

The archers fiercely attacked him, shot at him, and harassed him sorely; yet his bow remained unmoved, his arms were made agile by the hands of the ʾ*byr* of Jacob (by the name of the Shepherd, the Rock of Israel)

Ex 15:13–15

Thou hast led (*nḥyt* cf. Ps 77:21) in thy steadfast love the people whom thou hast redeemed, thou hast guided them by thy strength to thy holy abode (of shepherd or flocks—*nwh*). The peoples have heard, they tremble; pangs have seized on the inhabitants of Philistia. Now are the chiefs of Edom dismayed; the "rams" (ʾ*yly*) of Moab, trembling seizes them ...

Num 27:16, 17, 21

Let the Lord, the God of the spirits of all flesh, appoint a man over the congregation, who shall *go out before them and come in before them, who shall lead them out and bring them in*; that the congregation of the Lord may not be as *sheep which have no shepherd.*

And he shall stand before Eleazar the priest, who shall inquire for him by the

---

[60] Lang, Leaf and Myers n.d., 78–79 (Book V).
[61] Lang, Leaf and Myers n.d., 32–33 (Book II).
[62] Lang, Leaf and Myers n.d., 50 (Book III).
[63] Lang, Leaf and Myers n.d., 239–240 (Book XIII).

judgment of the Urim before the Lord; *at his word they shall go out, and at his word they shall come in*, both he and all the people of Israel with him, the whole congregation.

1 Sam 18:13, 16

So Saul removed him from his presence, and made him a commander of a thousand; and *he went out and came in before the people*.

But all Israel and Judah loved David; for *he went out and came in before them*.

2 Sam 5:2

In times past, when Saul was king over us, it was you that *led out and brought in Israel*; and the Lord said to you, You shall be *shepherd* of my people Israel, and you shall be prince over Israel.

1 Sam 21:8

Now a certain man of the servants of Saul was there that day, detained before the Lord; his name was Doeg the Edomite, the *ʾbyr* of Saul's *rᶜym*.

1 Kings 20:27

And the people of Israel were mustered, and were provisioned, and went against them; the people of Israel encamped before them like *two little flocks of goats*, but the Syrians filled the country.

1 Kings 22:11, 17 =2 Chron 18:10, 16

And Zedekiah the son of Chenaanah made for himself horns of iron, and said, Thus says the Lord, With these you shall push the Syrians until they are destroyed.

And he said, I saw all Israel scattered upon the mountains, as *sheep that have no shepherd*; and the Lord said, These have no master; let each return to his home in peace.

Isa 34:6–7; Eze 39:18, 20

The Lord has a sword; it is sated with blood, it is gorged with fat, with the blood of *lambs and goats*, with the fat of the kidneys of *rams*. For the Lord has a sacrifice in Bozrah, a great slaughter in the land of Edom. *Wild oxen* shall fall with them, and *young steers* with the *mighty bulls*.

You shall eat the flesh of *the mighty*, and drink the blook of *the princes of the earth*—of *rams*, of *lambs*, and of *goats*, of *bulls*, all of them *fatlings of Bashan*.

And you shall be filled at my table with *horses and riders, with mighty men and all kinds of warriors*, says the Lord God.

Jer 6:3, 4

Shepherds with their flocks shall come against her; they *shall pitch their tents around her, they shall pasture*, each in his place. *Prepare war against her*; up, and let us attack at noon!

Jer 12:10

Many shepherds have destroyed my vineyard, they have trampled down my portion, they have made my pleasant portion a desolate wilderness.

Mic 5:4–5, 7–8

And this shall be peace, when the Assyrian comes into our land and treads upon our soil, that we will raise against him *seven shepherds and eight princes of men; they shall rule (r⁼w) the land of Assyria with the sword*, and the land of Nimrod with the drawn sword; and they shall deliver us from the Assyrian when he comes into our land and treads within our border.

And the remnant of Jacob shall be among the nations, in the midst of many peoples, like a lion among the beasts of the forest, *like a young lion among the flocks of sheep*, which, when it goes through, treads down and tears in pieces, and there is none to deliver. *Your hand shall be lifted up over your adversaries, and all your enemies shall be cut off.*

Nah 3:18

Your shepherds are asleep, O king of Assyria; your nobles slumber. *Your people are scattered on the mountains with none to gather them.*

Ps 44:6, 10–13, 23–24

Through thee we push down our foes; through thy name we tread down our assailants.

Yet thou hast cast us off and abased us, and *hast not gone out with our armies*. Thou hast made us turn back from the foe; and our enemies have gotten spoil. *Thou hast made us like sheep for slaughter*, and hast scattered us among the nations. Thou hast sold thy people for a trifle, demanding no high price for them.

Nay, for thy sake we are slain all the day long, and accounted as *sheep for the slaughter*. Rouse thyself! Why sleepest thou, O Lord? Awake! Do not cast us off for ever!

Ps 80:2

Give ear, O *Shepherd of Israel, thou who leadest Joseph like a flock*! Thou who art enthroned upon the cherubim, shine forth[64]

d. *Apocalyptic warrior shepherds.* As noted above, references to herd leaders in 1 Enoch 89–90 and Test Jos 19:6–9 occur in a military context. Similarly, the ten-horned beast, the ram and the he-goat of Daniel 7 and 8, which we have already identified as herd leaders or shepherds, are all depicted as fighting beasts representing warrior kings (7:7, 21, 23; 8:4–14, 20–25).

Although the horned beasts of Daniel 7 and 8 are nowhere specifically accompanied by fighting flocks, such might nonetheless still be implied. In Dan 7:17, 23; 8:20–22, for example, beasts or horns represent both kings and kingdoms, while in 1 En 89:47, the fight there depicted between the rams

---

[64] Cf. Miller (1973, 78) who notes that Ps 80:2 in its context is a call for victory in battle.

Saul and David clearly describes the engagement of two herd leaders, even though the flock over which each is placed is only specifically referred to in the previous verses (vss. 42–46). Already in Jer 50:17, a single sheep represents the whole flock:

Israel is a hunted (*pzwrh*) sheep (*śh*) driven away by lions. First the king of Assyria devoured him, and now at last Nebuchadrezzar king of Babylon has gnawed his bones.

Although *śh* means "one of a flock," *pzwrh* ("scattered") implies that the whole flock Israel is considered (cf. Jer 50:6). The absence of accompanying flocks in Daniel 7 and 8, therefore, does not contradict our identification of the horned beasts in these chapters as warrior shepherds or herd leaders.

(3) The warrior is the (destructive) SHEPHERD of the enemy

In Zech 11:4–6 and Ps 44:10, 12–13, gentile shepherd warriors "purchase" the flock Israel in order to slay her:

Zech 11:4–6	*Ps 44:10, 12–13*
Thus said the Lord my God: Become shepherd of *the flock doomed to slaughter.* *Those who buy them slay them and go unpunished; and those who sell them say, Blessed be the Lord, I have become rich*; and their own shepherds have no pity on them. For I will no longer have pity on the inhabitants of this land, says the Lord. Lo, I will cause men to fall each into the hand of his shepherd, and each into the hand of his king; and they shall crush the earth, and I will deliver none from their hand.	Yet thou hast cast us off and abased us, and hast not gone out with our armies ... Thou hast made us like *sheep for slaughter*, and hast scattered us among the nations. *Thou hast sold thy people for a trifle, demanding no high price for them.*

In both passages, trading and slaughtering practices taken from pastoral life describe military engagements.

Military notions also underlie the use of *r^{c}h* meaning "destroy" in Jer 2:16; 6:3; Mic 5:5 and Ps 80:14. Just as a shepherd's flock crops the grass of the field, so the warrior destroys the enemy. This idea also informs the horned-beast metaphors describing Israel in the Balaam cycle (Num 22:4 and 24:8), which in turn warrant comparison with Daniel 7's description of the ten-horned beast:

Num 22:4; 24:8	Dan 7:7, 23
And Moab said to the elders of Midian, This horde will now lick up all that is round about us, *as the ox licks up the grass of the field.*	
God brings him out of Egypt; he has as it were the *horns* of the wild ox, he shall *eat up the nations* his adversaries, and shall *break* their bones *in pieces*, and pierce them through with his arrows.	a fourth beast terrible and dreadful and exceedingly strong; and it had great iron teeth; it *devoured and broke in pieces*, and stamped the residue with its feet ... and it had ten *horns.* [the fourth kingdom] shall *devour the whole earth*, and trample it down, and *break it to pieces.*

Both Num 24:8 and Dan 7:7, 23 depict a military power as a horned beast which devours its enemies and breaks them in pieces, and reference in Num 22:4 to the ox which "licks up the grass of the field" would suggest that both the devouring wild ox and the devouring ten-horned beast "graze" their enemies as grass.

(4) *The ruler is the SHEPHERD of the nation*

In Zech 10:3; 11:4f., rulers are referred to as "shepherds." The idea of the shepherd ruler has a long history, and is widely attested in Mesopotamian, Egyptian, Greek and Israelite texts. Further OT references include 2 Sam 5:2; Isa 44:28; Jer 3:15; 10:21; 22:22; 23:1–4; 25:34–38; 50:6; Ezekiel 34; 37:24; Ps 78:70–72.

Having identified the horned beasts of Daniel 7 and 8 as herd leaders, it may be inferred that the kings they represent are shepherd rulers. In Part II, however, we noted that all the beasts of both chapters betray anomalous physical characteristics typical of Mesopotamian birth omens. Is it accurate to regard such anomalies as symbols for shepherd kings? Grounds for such a conclusion are to be found in various Mesopotamian, Jewish apocalyptic and Christian apocalyptic texts depicting shepherd rulers as animal anomalies:

a. *Šulgi*. Reference to Šulgi in the apodosis of an old Babylonian text belonging to the *Šumma izbu* series (YOS 10 56 41) invites the following comparisons, which indicate that the shepherd king of Sumer repeatedly depicted himself as a birth anomaly:

Šulgi

D 2–3 Shepherd Šulgi, the great bull with powerful limbs, the dragon with *eyes of a lion*! Young bull, born in the rich enclosure, thriving (?) there![65]

A 2–5 I, Šulgi, a mighty man from (the day) I was born am I, A fierce-eyed *lion*, born of the *ushumgal* am I, *King of the four corners* (of the universe) am I, Herdsman, shepherd of the black-heads am I ...[66]

C 6 I am the calf of a white cow, *with thick neck*, reared in the cow pen.[67]

C 2 I, Šulgi, I, the *Wild Bull* of extraordinary vigour, I, the *Lion* with wide open mouth![68]

D 6 Fierce *panther*, who feeds on rich milk, rampant bull, who was born to be a great beast![69]

Šumma izbu

X 39' If an anomaly's *eyes are (like) a lion's*—the prince will have no opponent.

VII 2 If an anomaly has the head of a *lion*, and the tail of a *lion*—*the prince will rule the four quarters*.

VII 69' If an anomaly's *neck is a solid block*—the prince will have auxiliary troops, and they will act on his orders.
VII 70' If an anomaly's *neck* and head are *massive*—the prince will become powerful.

XIX 18' If a cow gives birth and (the calf) has the head of a *lion*—[...]

V 96 If a ewe gives birth to a *leopard*—a prince will seize universal kingship.

b. *Herd leaders and the multiple-horned crown.* As Seibert has noted (see above), Mesopotamian texts identifying shepherd gods and shepherd kings with herd leaders provide the rationale for the multiple-horned crown worn by human-faced oxen in Mesopotamian art. Since the multiple-horned crown was also worn by composite beasts such as the Assyrian *lamassu* (see above), it is probable that the multiplicity of the horns no less than the hybrid forms of the *lamassu* reflects Mesopotamian divination notions.[70]

   c. *Jewish and Christian apocalyptic texts.* Finally, in both Jewish and Christian apocalyptic texts comparable to Daniel 7 and 8 and *Šumma izbu* (see Chapter Two), animal anomalies represent shepherd rulers. The uni-

---

[65] Klein 1968, 80.
[66] Pritchard (ed.) 1969, 584.
[67] Castellino 1972, 249.
[68] Castellino 1972, 249.
[69] Klein 1968, 81.
[70] Cf. above, n. 46.

corned ram in 1 En 90:9 represents Judas, the herd leader of the hosts of Israel; the anomaly born to the virgin in Test Jos 19:8 is a messianic shepherd figure who delivers "the bulls and the cow and the three horns" from the wild beasts (vss. 8–9), while the lamb with seven horns and seven eyes in Rev 5:6 is referred to in 7:17 as both king and shepherd. Such being the case, we may conclude that the horned anomalies of Daniel 7 and 8, which we have identified as herd leaders, are in fact, representative of shepherd rulers.

B. Prophetic sources

(5) God/Michael is the SHEPHERD of the angels

As I looked this horn made war with the saints, and prevailed over them (Dan 7:21).

It grew great, even to the host of heaven; and some of the host of the stars it cast down to the ground, and trampled upon them. It magnified itself, even up to the Prince of the host.

Then I heard a holy one speaking; and another holy one said to the one that spoke, For how long is the vision concerning the continual burnt offering, the transgression that makes desolate, and the giving over of the sanctuary and host to be trampled under foot? (Dan 8:10–11, 13).

The saints of Dan 7:21 and the starry host of Dan 8:10–11, 13 are the heavenly armies who form common cause with Israel, the "people of the saints" (7:27; 8:24).[71] In both Daniel 7 and 8, these celestial beings are attacked by a horned beast, while in Dan 8:10, 13, the fate of the heavenly host recalls the defeat of the ram in v. 7: both are cast down to the ground and trampled upon by the he-goat or its horn. Such imagery suggests that the angelic hosts in both chapters are regarded as warrior flocks.[72] The notion of celestial flocks or herds is preserved in the following texts (Mesopotamian, Egyptian, OT, apocalyptic):

a. *Mesopotamian heavenly flocks:*
Shepherd of that beneath, keeper of that above,
You, Šamaš, direct, you are the light of everything.[73]

Thou, Mullil, ... the shepherd of the black-headed,
Thou wild bull, who leads the hosts, thou, the ruler,
the godly wild bull of the upper and lower world ...![74]

---

[71] This point is argued in detail in Collins 1977, 123–147.
[72] Cf. Chapter Three above, n. 3.
[73] Lambert 1960, 129 (lines 33–34).
[74] Witzel 1935, 169 (Nr. 13).

86

b. *Egyptian heavenly herds:*

Oh (Osiris) NN, may Mechenti-irti protect you, your shepherd who is behind your calves.[75]

See, he has come! See, he has come! See, your brother has come! See, Mechenti-irti has come! (Also) when you don't recognize him, then you sleep in his embrace. When your discharge is disposed of, he is like your calf, like your shepherd.[76]

(Oh Osiris NN ...) you don't know them and delight over them. You have taken them into your embrace as the shepherd takes your calves.[77]

Commenting on these passages, Müller notes: "So ist offensichtlich an allen Stellen der Vergleich mit dem Hirten an eine bestimmte Handlung des Mechenti-irti gebunden, der die Sterne wie ein Hirt seine Kälber in die Arme schliesst."[78]

c. *OT heavenly herds and flocks:*

Job 38:31–32
Can you *bind the chains* of the Pleiades, or *loose the cords* of Orion? Can you *lead forth* the Mazzaroth in their season, or can you *guide* the Bear *with its children*?

The expressions "bind the chains" and "loose the cords" allude to the pastoral practice of yoking and unyoking cattle.[79] Similarly, the expressions "lead forth" and "guide ... with its children" depict Yahweh as shepherd of the stars (cf. Isa 40:11).

Ps 147:2–4
The Lord builds up Jerusalem; he gathers the outcasts of Israel. He heals the brokenhearted, and binds up their wounds. He determines the number of the stars, he gives to all of them their names.

Here Yahweh as shepherd of heaven and earth gathers (cf. Isa 56:8), heals, and binds up the wounds (cf. Eze 34:4) of his earthly flock, and numbers (cf. Jer 33:13) and names (cf. John 10:3) the stars of heaven.

Isa 40:26
Lift up your eyes on high and see: who created these? He who brings out their host by number, calling them all by name; by the greatness of his might, and because he is strong in power not one is missing.

---

[75] Müller 1961, 128 (Pyr 771 a–b).
[76] Müller 1961, 128 (Pyr 1864a–1865b).
[77] Müller 1961, 128 (Pyr 1533 a–b).
[78] Müller 1961, 129.
[79] Cf. Büchler 1967, 71–72; Isa 58:6; Hos 11:3–4; Zad Frag 16:3.

Exegetes such as Mowinckel[80] and North[81] have noted the pastoral imagery underlying this verse, which closely resembles Ps 147:4.

Isa 34:2, 4–7

For the Lord is enraged against all the nations, and furious against all their *host*, he has doomed them, has given them over for *slaughter*.

All the host of heaven shall rot away, and the skies roll up like a scroll. All their host shall fall, as leaves fall from the vine, like leaves falling from the fig tree. *For my sword has drunk its fill in the heavens*; behold, it descends for judgment upon Edom, upon the people I have doomed. The Lord has a sword; it is sated with blood, it is gorged with fat, with the blood of *lambs and goats*, with the fat of the kidneys of *rams*. For the Lord has a sacrifice in Bozrah, a great slaughter in the land of Edom. *Wild oxen* shall fall with them, and *young steers* with the *mighty bulls*. Their land shall be soaked with blood, and their soil made rich with fat.

According to these verses, both heavenly and earthly hosts fall common victims to Yahweh's sacrificial sword. The stars, no less than the warriors of Edom, are consequently regarded as horned beasts.

d. *Apocalyptic heavenly herds and flocks:*

1 En 86:1, 3

And again I looked with my eyes as I was sleeping, and I saw heaven above, and behold, a star fell from heaven, and it arose and ate and pastured amongst those bulls.

And again I saw in the vision and looked at heaven, and behold, I saw many stars, how they came down and were thrown down from heaven to that first star, and amongst those heifers and bulls; they were with them, pasturing amongst them.

This passage is of interest, since it indicates that the notion of heavenly herds was familiar to apocalyptic circles in the Maccabean period.

In Dan 8:10, 11, 13, the stars attacked by the little horn are referred to as the "host" (*ṣbʾ*). Since the term is already used in connection with celestial flocks or herds in Isa 34:2f. and 40:26 (see above), it is probable that *ṣbʾ* in Daniel 8 refers to the warrior flock belonging to the heavenly prince of v. 11. In Dan 10:21 this prince is referred to as Michael,[82] in a passage reminiscent of Isa 63:9. Nickelsburg notes the similarities between the figures described in these two passages:

The general form of the epiphany is the same. The unnamed figure in Is. 63 says that he has *fought alone*, with *none* to help, *none* to uphold (vv. 3, 5). Therefore he has brought victory. Verse 9 tells how *the angel of the presence helped* Israel in the

---

[80] Noted in Muilenburg 1956, 442.
[81] North 1952, 47.
[82] Cf. Lacocque 1979, 162.

Exodus. The unnamed figure in Dan. 10 says, "... what is inscribed in the book of truth: there is *none who contends* by my side against these *except Michael* your prince" (v. 21).[83]

The pericope Isa 63:7–64:11, however, is a communal lament addressed to Israel's shepherd God (63:11–14), and is occasioned by the destruction of the temple and its aftermath (63:18; 64:10–11). The hope expressed in this passage that Yahweh or his shepherd angel (Isa 63:9 cf. 40:11) might deliver Israel from those defiling the temple appears anew in Daniel 8–12, where Michael the prince of the heavenly flock (8:11 cf. 10:21) delivers Israel from Antiochus, the little horn of the he-goat (8:25; 12:1).

(6) *The ruler is the SHEPHERD of the temple*
and the place of his sanctuary was overthrown ...

Then I heard a holy one speaking; and another holy one said to that one that spoke, For how long is the vision concerning the continual burnt offering, the transgression that makes desolate, and the giving over of the sanctuary and host to be trampled under foot? And he said to him, For two thousand and three hundred evenings and mornings; then the sanctuary shall be restored to its rightful state (Dan 8:11, 13–14).

The vision of the desecration of the sanctuary and its ultimate restoration betrays clear continuities with the vision of the ram and he-goat. Like the ram, the sanctuary is cast down and trampled underfoot by the he-goat or its horn (cf. v. 7). The ram image thereby "filters" the reader's perception of the sanctuary, which falls to the he-goat's onslaughts in the manner of a horned beast.[84] Moreover, a contrast is probably intended between vss. 7 and 14: whereas "there was no one who could rescue" the ram from the he-goat (v. 7 cf. also v. 4), the sanctuary is in fact restored (v. 14) in response to the lament of v. 13.

The expression "there was no one who could rescue," here used in connection with fighting beasts as military symbols (vss. 4, 7), suggests the absence of a shepherd (cf. Mic 5:7; Nah 3:18; Eze 34:6; Isa 5:29; Hos 5:14; 1 QSb V 29). It is therefore possible that the one rescuing the sanctuary from the power of the little horn in v. 14 is shepherd of the temple.[85] Both in

---

[83] Nickelsburg 1972, 21.

[84] Cf. Chapter Three above, n. 3.

[85] Pastoral metaphors for temples are highly developed in both Mesopotamian and OT texts. Numerous Sumerian hymns refer to the temple as either a cattle pen or a horned beast (see Sjöberg, Bergmann and Gragg 1969, 23, 26, 27, 33, 44, 167–170), while in the Psalter, "the sheep of his pasture" is a regular term for the worshipping community (Ps 74:1; 79:13; 95:7; 100:3). The term *nwh* ("abode of shepherd or flocks") is poetically applied to temples in 2 Sam 15:25; Isa 33:20; Jer 31:22; Ex 15:13; Jer 50:7, and in several instances, the pastoral connotations of the term are clearly preserved (Ex 15:13; Jer 31:22–23; Jer 50:6–7). Similarly, several OT passages refer to the temple as a mountain pasture for the flock (Ex 15:17; Isa 11:6–9;

Mesopotamia and in Israel, temple building or temple restoration is the responsibility of shepherd kings and gods. The following texts from various periods are representative:

a. *Mesopotamian texts:*

Gudea (ca. 2050 BCE)

My shepherd, I wish to explain your dream to you!

He has ordered you to build his *temple*, the Eninnu.[86]

good Shepherd Gudea,

Through the establishment of *my house*, abundance will come.[87]

The shepherd builds the house of precious metal.[88]

After Gudea had built the house, had finished the building,
The heart of the gods overflows with grace,
The good shepherd Gudea knows much and puts much into practice.[89]

I, the Shepherd, have built the house.[90]

Shamshi-Adad V (824–812 BCE)

Shamshi-Adad, the mighty king, the king of the universe, without a rival, guardian (*shepherd*) *of the sanctuaries*, scepter-bearer of sacred places, ruler of all lands, ...[91]

Ashurbanipal (668–627 BCE)

For Enlil, lord of the lands, his lord, Ashurbanipal, the obedient ruler (*shepherd*), the powerful king, king of the four regions (of the world), *has rebuilt the brick* (*work*) *of Ekur*, his beloved temple.[92]

Nebuchadrezzar (605/4–562 BCE)

to keep the land in order, to exercise the *shepherdship* over the people, to sustain the cult places, *renew the temples*.[93]

56:7–8; 65:25; Eze 20:40 (cf. v. 37); 34:25–26; Mic 4:1, 2, 6–8; Zeph 3:11–13), while in both the OT and the intertestamental literature, the temple becomes the focal point for the ingathering of the scattered flock (Isa 56:7–8; 60:7; Eze 34:13; 37:21, 24, 26–28; Pss Sol 17:26–28, 32–33, 45–46; 1 En 90:33).

[86] Falkenstein 1953, 142 (lines 11, 18).
[87] Falkenstein 1953, 148 (lines 5, 10–11).
[88] Falkenstein 1953, 154 (line 24).
[89] Falkenstein 1953, 162 (lines 21–24).
[90] Falkenstein 1953, 167 (line 3).
[91] Luckenbill 1927, 1:254.
[92] Luckenbill 1927, 2:405.
[93] Engnell 1967, 42.

Enlil (neo-Sumerian—ca 2060–1950 BCE)
You built the city Nippur by yourself.
The Ki'ur, your pure place, . . . ,
In the Duranki, in the middle of the four quarters of the earth, you founded it.
Its soil is the life of the land (Sumer), the life of all the foreign lands.
Its brickwork is gleaming gold, its foundation is lapislazuli.
Like a steer, it raises up its horns in Sumer

Enlil, *faithful shepherd* of everything that multiplies,
Shepherd, the leader of living creatures[94]

b. *OT and intertestamental texts:*

David/Solomon

In all places where I have moved with all the people of Israel, did I speak a word with any of the judges of Israel, *whom I commanded to shepherd my people Israel, saying, Why have you not built me a house of cedar?* Now therefore thus you shall say to my servant David, Thus says the Lord of hosts, *I took you from the pasture, from following the sheep*, that you should be a prince over my people, Israel.

When your days are fulfilled and you lie down with your fathers, I will raise up your offspring after you, who shall come forth from your body, and I will establish his kingdom. *He shall build a house for my name*, and I will establish the throne of his kingdom for ever (2 Sam 7:7–8, 12–13).

Cyrus

who says of Cyrus, He is my *shepherd*, and he shall fulfil all my purpose; saying of Jerusalem, She shall be built, *and of the temple, Your foundation shall be laid* (Isa 44:28).

Yahweh

He rejected the tent of Joseph, he did not choose the tribe of Ephraim; but he chose the tribe of Judah, Mount Zion, which he loves. *He built his sanctuary* like the high heavens, like the earth, which he has founded for ever. *He chose David his servant, and took him from the sheepfolds; from tending the ewes that had young he brought him to be the shepherd of Jacob his people*, of Israel his inheritance. *With upright heart he tended them, and guided them with skilful hand* (Ps 78:67–72).

My servant David shall be king over them; and they shall all have one *shepherd*.

. . . and I will bless them and multiply them, and will set my *sanctuary* in the midst of them for evermore. My dwelling place shall be with them; and I will be their God, and they shall be my people. Then the nations will know that I the Lord sanctify Israel, when my *sanctuary* is in the midst of them for evermore (Eze 37:24, 26–28).

And I looked until *the Lord of the sheep brought a new house*, larger and higher than that first one, and he set it up on the site of the first one which had been folded up; and all its pillars (were) new, and its ornaments (were) new and larger than (those of) the first one, the old one which he had removed. And the Lord of the sheep (was) in the middle of it (1 En 90:29).

---

[94] Reisman 1969, 62–63 (lines 66–71, 93–94).

Comparable to the lament for the sanctuary in Dan 8:13 with its attendant pastoral imagery are the communal laments Psalm 74, Psalm 79 and Isa 63:7–64:11. All three passages lament the destruction of the temple (Ps 74:3f.; 79:1; Isa 63:18; 64:10–11), and all are addressed to the shepherd God (Ps 74:1, 4, 19; Ps 79:7 (*nwh*), 13; Isa 63:9, 11–14). Daniel 8's allusion to the sanctuary as a horned beast (vss. 11, 13) however, is most strikingly antici-pated in two Sumerian laments: the *Lamentation over the Destruction of Ur*,[95] and the *Lamentation over the Destruction of Sumer and Ur*.[96] Al-though both works are much earlier than OT laments for Jerusalem, a degree of similarity cannot be disputed.[97] As in the OT laments for Jerusalem and the temple, pastoral imagery features prominently in these two works. Lines 263–266 of the *Lamentation over the Destruction of Ur* depict the city and its temple complex as a sheep forsaken by its shepherd:

My houses of the outer city verily have been destroyed—"alas for my city" I will say;
My houses of the inner city verily have been destroyed—"alas for my house" I will say;
My city like an innocent ewe has not been . . .ed, *gone is its trustworthy shepherd*;
Ur like an innocent ewe has not been . . .ed, *gone is its shepherd boy.*[98]

Similarly, lines 52–54 and 262 of the *Lamentation over the Destruction of Sumer and Ur* refer to the temple city as a prostrated warrior ox:

That *Ur, the great wild ox* which steps forth confidently (in combat), which is secure in its own strength,
My city of lordship and kingship, built on pure soil,
Like an ox to be thrown instantly by the nose-rope, be fastened neck to ground

Ur, the great wild ox that (formerly) stepped forth confidently (in combat), *has been made prostrate.*[99]

Passages such as these emphasize the shepherd's responsibility for the upkeep of temples and cities by taking the additional step of describing the temple or temple city as a horned beast.[100] Similar notions appear in a Sumerian vase inscription of Lugalzaggisi, king of Uruk:

In the sanctuaries of Sumer as *patesi* of the lands and in Erech as priest of the highest they appointed him. When Erech with gladness he had made bright, *Ur like an ox its head to heaven he raised, Larsa* the city beloved by Utu *with waters of joy he*

---

[95] Pritchard (ed.) 1950, 455–463.
[96] Pritchard (ed.) 1969, 611–619.
[97] Beyerlin (ed.) 1978, 116.
[98] Pritchard (ed.) 1950, 460.
[99] Pritchard (ed.) 1969, 613, 616.
[100] For further instances of cattle of sheep imagery applied to Sumerian temples, see already notes 85 and 94 above.

watered; Umma the city beloved by Shara to great power he raised; *Kininniesh like a pregnant ewe in a watered enclosure he restored her fatness*; the place of heaven and earth, to the height of heaven he restored.

The shepherd who lifts up the head of the ox may he be forever![101]

It may be assumed that the author of Daniel 8 was familiar with imagery of this sort. Interest in old traditions was strong throughout the Hellenistic world, and a lament for Uruk, composed in the third millennium BCE, is known to have been recopied in the early Hellenistic period, after Babylon was overrun by foreigners. [102] Moreover, in the following complaints to the shepherd god Enlil copied during the Seleucid period, his city is apparently referred to as a destroyed sheep or ox:

The great mountain, father Enlil, lies down dreaming.
The shepherd of the black-headed lies down dreaming.

The sheep residing in the sheepfold lies down dreaming.
The eminent one, you have given away your city and it is
instantly devoured. [103]

Umunirigalla, raise your hands!

Your city, *(the city of) thick horns*, he (Enlil) has destroyed. The great strength of your city he has destroyed. [104]

Daniel 8's pastoral metaphor for the temple consequently presupposes the OT and ancient Near Eastern notion of the king as shepherd of the temple. Allusion to the temple as a horned beast is reminiscent of imagery occurring in Mesopotamian laments from Sumerian times to the Seleucid period, and it may be supposed that Daniel's temple imagery ultimately stems from sources of this kind. [105]

(7) God is the SHEPHERD of truth

and truth was cast down to the ground (Dan 8:12).

According to this verse, truth, like the ram in v. 7, is cast down to the ground by the he-goat. [106] In the communal lament Isa 59:1–15a, the complaint is made that "truth has fallen (*kšlh*) in the public squares" (v. 14), and

---

[101] Barton 1929, 99.

[102] Pinches 1908, 477–478; Collins 1977, 102.

[103] Cohen 1972, 337 (lines 23', 28'–29').

[104] Cohen 1972, 136 (lines 93, 95–96).

[105] Cf. also reference to Jerusalem as a fighting horned beast in Mic 4:13: "Arise and thresh, O daughter of Zion, for I will make your horn iron and your hoofs bronze; you shall beat in pieces many peoples, and shall devote their gain to the Lord, their wealth to the Lord of the whole earth."

[106] Cf. Chapter Three above, n. 3.

it is probable that the author of Daniel 8 has drawn from this source.[107] As the following comparison indicates, the use of *kšl* in connection with "truth" in this verse is to be explained in the light of the "path" metaphor of vss. 7–10:

Isa 59:7–10

Their feet run to evil, and they
make haste to shed innocent blood;
their thoughts are thoughts of
iniquity, desolation and
destruction are in their high-
ways.
The way of peace they know not,
and there is no justice (mšpṭ)
in their paths; they have made
their roads crooked, no one
who goes in them knows peace.
Therefore *justice (mšpṭ)* is far
from us, and *righteousness (ṣdqh)*
does not overtake us ...
... we stumble *(kšlnw)* at noon as
in the twilight ...

Isa 59:14

Justice (mšpṭ) is turned back,
and *righteousness (ṣdqh)* stands
afar off; for truth has *fallen*
(kšlh) in the public squares,
and uprightness cannot enter.

Both Israel and truth "stumble" (Isa 59:10, 14) because the roads prepared by the wicked are crooked (v. 8). The pastoral connotations of the metaphor emerge in Jer 31:8–9:

With weeping they shall come, and with consolations I will lead them back, I will make them walk by brooks of water, *in a straight path in which they shall not stumble (ykšlw)*; for I am a father to Israel, and Ephraim is my first-born. Hear the word of the Lord, O nations, and declare it in the coastlands afar off: say, He who scattered Israel will gather him, and will keep him as a *shepherd keeps his flock*.

Similarly, in Isa 63:11, 13 and Pss Sol 17:45, it is the righteous shepherd who saves his flock from stumbling:

... Where is he who brought up out of the sea the shepherds of *his flock*?

who led them through the depths? Like a horse in the desert, they did not *stumble (ykšlw)*.

(He will be) *shepherding* the flock of the Lord faithfully and righteously, And will suffer none among them to *stumble* in their pasture.

Finally, in Ps 23:1, 3, Yahweh the shepherd leads his sheep in "paths of rigtheousness" (*mᶜgly ṣdq* —cf. *mᶜgl ... ṣdqh*, Isa 59:8–9).

---

[107] Nickelsburg 1972, 21.

The Lord is my *shepherd*, I shall not want.

... He leads me in *paths of righteousness* for his name's sake.

Isa 59:14 consequently describes the collapse of justice in Israel by likening truth to a sheep that has stumbled in Israel's public squares, which have become as the crooked paths of the wicked.[108] That the sheep metaphor is active in this verse is further indicated by the imagery of v. 15:

Truth is lacking (*n ʿdrt*), and he who departs from evil makes himself a prey.

The root *ʿdr* is the same as that from which the word "flock" is formed, and in Isa 40:26, the *niphʿal* form is used of Yahweh's heavenly flock:

Lift up your eyes on high and see: who created these? He who brings out their host by number, calling them all by name; by the greatness of his might, and because he is strong in power not one is missing (*n ʿdr*).

Reference to the "prey" in Isa 59:15 completes the pastoral metaphor. Because truth has "stumbled" in the crooked paths, it is "lacking" or missing from the flock, and followers of truth have become a "prey." The complaint is consequently addressed to Yahweh the shepherd, who, as ruler of Israel, must rescue her from her state of fallen justice.

C. Psalmodic sources

(8) *The judge is the SHEPHERD of the oppressed*

In Daniel 7, the saints secure the kingdom in a court scene in which the Ancient of Days passes judgment on the four beasts. Forensic deliverance from wild beasts is also depicted in the following laments in the Psalter: Psalms 7, 10, 17, 35, 22, 59, 58, 74.[109] Since the animals in such laments probably came to represent Israel's foreign overlords during the exilic/post-exilic period,[110] comparison of these psalms with Daniel 7 is warranted.

Individual laments:

Ps 7:2–3, 7–9
O Lord my God, in thee do I take refuge; save me from all my pursuers, and deliver me, lest like a *lion* they rend me, dragging me away, with none to rescue.

Arise, O Lord, in thy anger, lift thyself up against the fury of my enemies; awake, O

---

[108] Cf. the Palestinian proverb, "Truth is a butting (ox)," noted in Stephan 1925, 100.
[109] The psalms of lament are more stereotyped than any other group in the Psalter, and those containing forensic allusions doubtless served in varying contexts as the need arose.
[110] See n. 10 above.

my God; *thou hast appointed a judgment. Let the assembly of the peoples be gathered about thee; and over it take thy seat on high. The Lord judges the peoples; judge me, O Lord, according to my righteousness.*

Ps 10:9, 12, 13, 17, 18

he lurks in secret like a *lion* in his covert; he lurks that he may seize the poor, he seizes the poor when he draws him into his net.

Arise, O Lord; O God, lift up thy hand; forget not the afflicted. Why does the wicked renounce God, and say in his heart, Thou wilt not call to account?

O Lord, thou wilt hear the desire of the meek, thou wilt strengthen their heart, *thou wilt incline thy ear to do justice* to the fatherless and the oppressed, so that man who is of the earth may strike terror no more.

Ps 17:1, 2, 12, 13

Hear a just cause, O Lord; attend to my cry! Give ear to my prayer from lips free from deceit! *From thee let my vindication come!* Let thy eyes see the right!

They are like a lion eager to tear, as a young lion lurking in ambush. Arise, O Lord! Confront them, overthrow them! Deliver my soul from the wicked by thy sword

Ps 35:11, 16, 17, 21–25

Malicious witnesses rise up; they ask me of things that I know not.

they impiously mocked more and more, gnashing at me with their teeth. How long, O Lord, wilt thou look on? *Rescue me from their ravages, my life from the lions!*

They open wide their mouths against me; they say, Aha, Aha! our eyes have seen it! Thou hast seen, O Lord; be not silent! O Lord, be not far from me! Bestir thyself, and *awake for my right, for my cause,* my God and my Lord! *Vindicate me,* O Lord, my God, according to thy righteousness; and let them not rejoice over me! Let them not say to themselves, Aha, we have our heart's desire! Let them not say, *We have swallowed him up.*

Ps 22:13, 14, 17, 21, 22

Many *bulls* encompass me, strong *bulls* of Bashan surround me; they *open wide their mouths at me, like a ravening and roaring lion.*

Yea, *dogs* are round about me; a company of evildoers encircle me; they have pierced my hands and feet—

Deliver my soul from the sword, *my life from the power of the dog! Save me from the mouth of the lion,* my afflicted soul *from the horns of the wild oxen!*

The animal imagery of Psalm 22 is reminiscent of Psalm 35, where forensic themes are clearly indicated (see above). Compare Ps 22:14 ("they open wide their mouths at me") and Ps 35:21 ("They open wide their mouths against me"); Ps 22:22 ("Save me from the mouth of the lion") and Ps 35:17 ("Rescue me from their ravages, my life from the lions!"). Such parallels suggest a forensic interpretation of the animal imagery in Psalm 22, as in Psalm 35.

Ps 59:2, 7, 8, 13, 15, 16

Deliver me from my enemies, O my God, protect me *from those who rise up against me*

Each evening they come back, *howling like dogs* and prowling about the city. There they are, *bellowing with their mouths, and snarling with their lips* — for Who, they think, will hear us?

For the *sin of their mouths, the words of their lips*, let them be trapped in their pride. For the cursing and lies which they utter

Each evening they come back, *howling like dogs* and prowling about the city. They roam about for food, and growl if they do not get their fill.

Communal laments:

Ps 58:4–5, 7, 12

The wicked go astray from the womb, they err from their birth, speaking lies. They have venom like the venom of a *serpent*, like the deaf adder that stops its ear

O God, *break the teeth in their mouths; tear out the fangs of the young lions*, O Lord!

Men will say, Surely there is a reward for the righteous; *surely there is a God who judges on earth.*

Ps 74:4, 18–19, 22

Thy foes have *roared* in the midst of thy holy place ...

Remember this, O Lord, how the enemy scoffs, and an impious people reviles thy name. Do not deliver the soul of thy dove to *the wild beasts*: do not forget the life of thy poor for ever.

Arise, O God, plead thy cause; remember how the impious scoff at thee all the day!

Each of these laments depicts the psalmist's enemies as predators or horned beasts, against whom God is asked to intervene in judgment. Animals specifically mentioned or alluded to are lions (Ps 7:3; 10:9; 17:12; 22:14, 17, 22; 35:16, 17, 21, 25; 58:7; 74:4 cf. v. 19); dogs (Ps 22:17, 21; 59:7, 8, 15, 16); serpents (Ps 58:5); bulls (Ps 22:13); and wild oxen (Ps 22:22). Such are comparable to the predators and the horned beast which come into judgment in Daniel 7. As in Daniel 7, the judgment of the beasts in several of these laments is also associated with the idea or future hope of Yahweh's or Israel's sovereignty over the nations:

Psalms	*Daniel 7*
7:9 The Lord judges the peoples	v. 14 And to him was given dominion and glory and kingdom, that all peoples, nations, and
10:16 The Lord is king for ever and ever; the nations shall perish from his land	languages should serve him; his dominion is an everlasting dominion, which shall not pass away, and

22:28–30 All the ends of the
earth shall remember and turn
to the Lord; and all the families
of the nations shall worship
before him. For dominion belongs
to the Lord, and he rules over the
nations. Yea, to him shall all the
proud of the earth bow down; before him shall bow all who
go down to the dust, and he who
cannot keep himself alive.

59:6, 9 Thou, Lord God of hosts,
art God of Israel. Awake to
punish all the nations; spare
none of those who treacherously
plot evil.
But thou, O Lord, dost laugh at
them; thou dost hold all the
nations in derision.

his kingdom one that shall not
be destroyed.

v. 17 These four great beasts are four
kings who shall arise out of the
earth.

Pastoral imagery in the psalms of lament

Wild beast imagery in several of the above laments presupposes the notion
of Yahweh the shepherd judge, who delivers his sheep or flock from the
devouring enemy. In Psalm 74, for example, the victims of the wild beasts
are referred to as sheep (vss. 1, 4, 19):

O God, why dost thou cast us off for ever? Why does thy anger smoke against *the
sheep of thy pasture*?

Thy foes have *roared* in the midst of thy holy place . . .

Do not deliver the soul of thy dove to *the wild beasts* . . .[111]

Similarly, as the following comparisons indicate, various expressions concerning the deliverance of the oppressed in Psalms 7, 22 and 35 also suggest
the action of the faithful shepherd:

---

[111] A similar association of ideas occurs in the *Lament over the Destruction of Sumer and Ur*,
lines 189–190 (Pritchard (ed.) 1969, 615): "The settlements of the Edanna and Nanna were
destroyed like a distended stall, Those who fled from it were devoured by the wild beasts like
fleeing kids." The dove image (Ps 74:19) possibly underlines the helplessness of the attacked
flock. Cf. Merneptah's address to his court: "I am the ruler who shepherds you; I spend my
time searching out – – – – – you, as a father, who preserves alive his children; while ye fear like
birds, and ye know not the goodness of that which he does" (Breasted 1906–7, 3:243).

Ps 7:2–3, 6–7

O Lord my God, in thee do I
take refuge; save me from all my
pursuers, and deliver me
(*hṣylny*),
lest *like a lion* they rend me,
dragging me away, with *none to
rescue* (*ᵓyn mṣyl*).
let the enemy pursue me and
overtake me, and let him
trample (*yrms*) my life to the
ground, and lay my soul in the
dust.
Arise, O Lord, in thy anger,
lift thyself up against the
fury of my enemies; *awake*,
O my God; thou has appointed a
judgment.

Ps 22:22; 35:17[112]

Save me from the mouth of the
lion ...
Rescue me from their ravages,
my life from the lions!

Mic 5:7

And the remnant of Jacob shall
be among the nations, in the
midst of many peoples, like a
lion among the beasts of the
forest, *like a young lion* among
the flocks of sheep, which, when
it goes through, *treads down*
(*rms*) and tears in pieces, and
there is *none to deliver* (*ᵓyn mṣyl*)

Ps 44:23–24

Nay, for thy sake we are slain
all the day long, and accounted
as sheep for the slaughter.
Rouse thyself! *Why sleepest thou,
O Lord? Awake!* Do not cast us
off forever!

Nah 3:18

Your shepherds are asleep, O king
of Assyria; your nobles slumber.
Your people are scattered on the
mountains with none to gather
them.

Eze 34:10, 16

no longer shall the shepherds
feed themselves. *I will rescue
my sheep from their mouths*, that
they may not be food for them.
... I will feed them *in justice*.

1 Sam 17:34–35

when there came *a lion* or a bear,
and took a lamb from the flock,
I went after him and smote him
*and delivered it out of his
mouth*.

Amos 3:12

As the shepherd *rescues from the
mouth of the lion* ...

In each of these psalms, God is depicted as a shepherd judge, who delivers
the oppressed petitioner(s) from the wild beasts (the adversaries). Further

---

[112] Cf. also the hymn to Amon-Re quoted below (n. 117).

indications of the shepherd-judge metaphor are to be found in the following texts (Mesopotamian, Egyptian, OT, apocalyptic): [113]

a. *Mesopotamian shepherd judge:*

Šulgi

As a faithful shepherd who delights in justice.

.... what(ever) it was. I wanted to act against ...
[I, the king], *the shepherd*, took the (necessary) decision, with the will of ever since,
To give back to his (the shepherd's) people what the rebellious house had plundered, that was my success.
For (the restoration of) justice, as if they were great bulls, I got hold of the criminals,
And against the evil ones I acted, *as towards a serpent*, that when struck darts out its tongue.
For the just man to whom justice had not been provided, I [...]
For the rebel, that had not been placed into confinement, I [...][114]

Šamaš

Shepherd of that beneath, keeper of that above,
You, Šamaš, direct, you are the light of everything.

[.....] *you blaze abroad the judgments on the criminal and lawbreaker.*

What you say in a *just verdict*, Šamaš, [...]

A man who covets his neighbour's wife
Will [........] before his appointed day.
A nasty snare is prepared for him.. [........]
Your weapon will strike at him, and there [will be] none to save him.
[His] father will not stand for his defence,
And at the judge's command his brothers will not plead.
He will be caught in a copper trap that he did not foresee.
You destroy the horns of a scheming villain,
A zealous ...., his foundations are undermined.
You give the unscrupulous judge experience of fetters,
Him who accepts a present and yet lets justice miscarry you make bear his punishment. [115]

---

[113] For Rabbinic use of the metaphor (ca. 225 CE), cf. Ginzberg 1909–55, 4:16–17: "Moses, however, was still very much troubled in mind, on account of Samael, who had not left off lodging accusations before God against Israel since the exodus from Egypt. The Lord adopted the same procedure in dealing with the accuser as the experienced shepherd, who, at the moment of transferring his sheep across a stream, was faced by a ravening wolf. The shepherd threw a strong ram to the wolf, and while the two engaged in combat, the rest of the flock was carried across the water, and then the shepherd returned and snatched the wolf's supposed prey away from him. Samael said to the Lord: 'Up to this time the children of Israel were idol worshippers, and now Thou proposest so great a thing as dividing the sea for them?' What did the Lord do? He surrendered Job to Samael, saying, 'While he busies himself with Job, Israel will pass through the sea unscathed, and as soon as they are in safety, I will rescue Job from the hands of Samael.'"

[114] Castellino 1972, 253, 255 (lines 73–79).

[115] Lambert 1960, 129, 131, 133 (lines 33–34, 58, 63, 88–98).

Hammurabi

at that time Anum and Enlil named me
to promote the welfare of the people,
me, Hammurabi, the devout, god-fearing prince,
to cause justice to prevail in the land,
to destroy the wicked and the evil,
that the strong might not oppress the weak,
to rise like the sun over the black-headed (people),
and to light up the land.
Hammurabi, the shepherd, called by Enlil, am I

I, Hammurabi, the perfect king,
was not careless (or) neglectful of the black-headed (people),
whom Enlil had presented to me,
(and) *whose shepherding Marduk had committed to me;*
I sought out peaceful regions for them;
I overcame grievous difficulties;
I caused light to rise on them,
With the mighty weapon which Zababa and Inanna entrusted to me,
with the insight that Enki allotted to me,
with the ability that Marduk gave me,
I rooted out the enemy above and below;
I made an end of war;
I promoted the welfare of the land;
I made the peoples rest in friendly habitations;
I did not let them have anyone to terrorize them.
The great gods called me,
so I became *the beneficent shepherd whose scepter is righteous:*
my benign shadow is spread over my city.
In my bosom I carried the peoples of the land of Sumer and Akkad;
they prospered under my protection;
I have governed them in peace;
I have *sheltered* them in my strength.
In order that the strong might not oppress the weak,
that justice might be dealt the orphan (and) the widow.

If that man heeded my words which I wrote on my stela,
and did not scorn my law,
did not distort my words,
did not alter my statutes,
may Shamash make that man reign
as long as the king of justice:
may he shepherd his people in justice![116]

b. *Egyptian shepherd judge:*
O Amon, thou herdman bringing forth the herds in the morning, leading the suffer-
ing to pasture; as the herdman leads the herds [to] *pasture,* so dost thou, O Amon,
lead the suffering to food, for Amon is a herdman, herding him that leans upon

---

[116] Pritchard (ed.) 1950, 164, 177–178.

him .... O Amon-Re, I love thee and I have filled my heart with thee .... *Thou wilt rescue me out of the mouth of men in the day when they speak lies*; for the Lord of Truth, he liveth in truth. [117]

c. *OT shepherd judge:*

Isa 11:3–7

He shall not judge by what his eyes see, or decide by what his ears hear; but *with righteousness he shall judge the poor*, and decide with equity for the *meek* of the earth; and he shall smite the earth with the *rod of his mouth*, and with the breath of his lips he shall slay the wicked. Righteousness shall be the girdle of his waist, and faithfulness the girdle of his loins. The *wolf* shall dwell with the *lamb*, and the *leopard* shall *lie down* with the *kid*, and the *calf* and the *lion* and the *fatling* together, and a little child shall lead them. The *cow* and the *bear* shall *feed*; their young shall *lie down* together; and the *lion* shall eat straw like the *ox*.

Isa 14:30

And the first-born of the poor will *feed*, and the needy *lie down* in safety ...

Jer 33:13, 15

flocks shall again pass under the hand of the one who counts them, says the Lord.

In those days and at that time I will cause a righteous Branch to spring forth for David; and *he shall execute justice and righteousness* in the land.

Jer 49:19 = 50:44

Behold, *like a lion* coming up from the jungle of the Jordan *against a strong sheepfold*, I will suddenly make them run away from her; and I will appoint over her whomever I choose. For who is like me? *Who will summon me (into court—y⁽ᶜ⁾d* cf. Job 9:19)? *What shepherd can stand before me*?

Eze 20:35–37 (cf. Lev 27:32)

And I will bring you into the wilderness of the peoples, and there I will enter into judgment with you face to face. As I entered into judgment with your fathers in the wilderness of the land of Egypt, so *I will enter into judgment with you*, says the Lord God. *I will make you pass under the rod, and I will let you go in by number.*

And all the tithe of herds and flocks, every tenth animal of *all that pass under the herdsman's staff*, shall be holy to the Lord.

Eze 34:10–23

no longer shall the shepherds feed themselves. *I will rescue my sheep from their mouths* that they may not be food for them. For thus says the Lord God: Behold, I, I myself will search for my sheep, and will seek them out. As a shepherd seeks out his flock when some of his sheep have been scattered abroad, so will I seek out my sheep; and I will rescue them from all places where they have been scattered on a day of clouds and thick darkness. And I will bring them out from the peoples, and gather them from the countries, and will bring them into their own land; and I will

---

[117] Breasted 1912, 355 (British Museum Ostrakon, No. 5656a).

feed them on the mountains of Israel, by the fountains, and in all the inhabited places of the country. I will feed them with good pasture, and upon the mountain heights of Israel shall be their pasture; there they shall *lie down* in good grazing land, and on fat pasture they shall *feed* on the mountains of Israel. I myself will be the shepherd of my sheep, and I will make them lie down, says the Lord God. I will seek the lost, and I will bring back the strayed, and I will bind up the crippled, and I will strengthen the weak, and the fat and the strong I will watch over: *I will feed them in justice.* As for you, my flock, thus says the Lord God: Behold, *I judge between sheep and sheep, rams and he-goats.* Is it not enough for you to feed on the good pasture, that you must tread down with your feet the rest of your pasture; and to drink of clear water, that you must foul the rest with your feet? And must my sheep eat what you have trodden with your feet, and drink what you have fouled with your feet? Therefore, thus says the Lord God to them: *Behold, I, I myself will judge between the fat sheep and the lean sheep.* Because you push with side and shoulder and thrust at all the weak with your horns, till you have scattered them abroad, *I will save my flock, they shall no longer be a prey; and I will judge between sheep and sheep.* And I will set up over them one shepherd, my servant David, and he shall feed them: he shall feed them and be their shepherd.

d. *Apocalyptic shepherd judge.* In Daniel 7, the judgment of the beasts takes place when the books are opened before the Ancient of Days. As noted in Chapter Four, this passage is closely paralleled in 1 En 90:20, where the books are opened before the Lord of the sheep:

Dan 7:9–10	*1 En 90:20*
As I looked, thrones were placed, and one that was ancient of days took his seat ... the court sat in judgment, and the books were opened.	And I looked until a throne was set up in the pleasant land, and the Lord of the sheep sat on it; and they took all the sealed books and opened those books before the Lord of the sheep.

These books are to be compared with herding contracts made between sheep owners and shepherds in ancient Mesopotamia:

Postgate 1975, 1–9 (italics ours)	*1 Enoch 89:59–77; 90:14–32*
The background to such herding contracts ... can therefore be stated very briefly. By the nature of their work, shepherds cannot be supervised like other employees, and it was and still is customary for a shepherd to be entrusted with flocks on the understanding that he will be held responsible for them, but will receive renumeration accordingly. *A shepherd might work on his own, or if he*	*And he called seventy shepherds and cast off those sheep that they might pasture them; and he said to the shepherds and to their companions: Each one of you from now on is to pasture the sheep, and do whatever I command you.* *And I will hand them over to you duly numbered and will tell you which of them are to be destroyed and destroy them ...* And he called another and said

103

*accepted more sheep than he
could pasture himself, he might
employ "under-shepherds" ... to
look after the flocks. The owner
of the sheep might be a private
individual, but it could also
be a temple or the palace (i.e.
the state administration) ....*
The herding contracts with which
we are immediately concerned
were drawn up once a year, and
constitute the shepherd's
acknowledgement that he accepts
responsibility for the animals
listed on the tablet. Sometimes (and probably in fact
always) *the tablet is sealed
with the shepherd's seal, and
it was known as the "sealed
tablet"* ... this served as a basis
for adjusting accounts between
the owner and the shepherd when
the animals were counted and the
losses and growth determined at
the end of each year ....
Shearing is a springtime activity,
and it is obvious that our contracts were drawn up after the
shearing, when the animals
passed once more from their
owners to the shepherds who were
to pasture them. Naturally the
shepherds were expected to bring
the flocks in to the shearing at
the end of each year, and the
agreement will only have been
operative until then .... When
at the end of the year the
accounts were adjusted, an
allowance was made to the
shepherd for the animals which
had died naturally in the
course of the year .... However,
*any loss in excess of the agreed
ratio had of course to be made
good by shepherd .... His
prime responsibility was to
keep his flock together and
prevent animals from straying.*
If an animal was lost, he was

to him: Observe and see everything that the shepherds do
against these sheep, for they
will destroy from among them
more than I have commanded
them.
*And write down all the excess
and destruction which is
wrought by the shepherds, how
many they destroy at my command,
and how many they destroy of
their own volition; write down
against each shepherd individually
all that he destroys.*
And read out before me exactly
how many they destroy of their
own volition, and how many are
handed over to them for destruction, *that this may be a testimony
for me against them*, that I may
know all the deeds of the shepherds,
in order to hand them over (for
destruction), and may see what
they do, whether they abide by
my command which I have commanded
them, or not.
But they must not know this, and
you must not show (this) to them ...
but (only) write down against
each individual in his time
all that the shepherds destroy
and bring it all up to me.
And I looked until those shepherds
pastured at their time, *and they
began to kill and to destroy more
than they were commanded, and
they gave those sheep into the
hands of the lions ...*
And the shepherds and their
companions handed those sheep
over to all the animals that
they might devour them; each one
of them at his time received an
exact number, and (of) each one
of them after the other there
was written in a book how many
of them he destroyed.
*And each one killed and destroyed
more than was prescribed*, and
I began to weep and to moan

of course unable to produce its skin, and was obliged to replace it by another animal .... At Larsa the standard agreement between the state and its shepherds ran "*PN shall be answerable to the king* for ... and any loss which occurs" ... *Finally, the flock may have been reduced by legitimate demands made on the shepherd by its owner.* These probably consisted mostly of males for eating, and at least in the state flocks the procedure was similar to that for dead animals. When an animal was handed back by the shepherd, it was known as an "issue" ..., and a text was made out acknowledging its receipt. Hence Ammi-ṣaduqa instructs his shepherds to come to the shearing with "the sealed tablets for the sheep which you gave out as issues," ... which would then of course be deducted from the total to which the shepherd was held liable .... Pulling the threads together, we may reconstruct the stages of the annual accounting for a herding contract as follows. *The shepherd arrives as instructed by the owner for the shearing, bringing with him any pertinent tablets. The animals are counted, the results being probably noted down on another tablet. These figures are then compared with the data of the previous year's "sealed tablet which was made out after the shearing", and any tablets recording subsequent additions or subtractions are taken into account. The subtractions will have consisted of issues authorized by the owner, or of losses by death, duly confirmed by a receipt from the owner or relevant*

very much because of those sheep. And likewise in the vision I saw that one who wrote, how every day he wrote down each one which was destroyed by those shepherds, and (how) he brought up and presented and showed the whole book to the Lord of the sheep, everything that they had done, and all that each one of them had made away with, and all that they had handed over to destruction.
And the book was read out before the Lord of the sheep, and he took the book in his hand, and read it, *and sealed it*, and put it down ...
But the Lord of the sheep remained still until all the sheep were scattered abroad and had mixed with them, and they did not save them from the hand of the animals.
And that one who wrote the book brought it up, and showed it, and read (it) out in the dwelling of the Lord of the sheep; and he entreated him on behalf of them, and petitioned him as he showed him all the deeds of their shepherds and testified before him against all the shepherds. And he took the book, and put it down by him, and went out. And I looked until that man who wrote down the names of the shepherds and brought (them) up before the Lord of the sheep came, and he helped that ram and showed it everything, namely, that its help was coming down. And I looked until that Lord of the sheep came to them in anger, and all those who saw him fled, and they all fell into the shadow before him ... And I looked at that man who ...

authorities for the skins,
etc .... At this point we have
reached the stage described by
a Larsa document as "issues
and losses have been deducted
and there is no replacement to
be made" ..., and at this stage
any animals surplus to the
agreed totals fall to the
shepherd. No doubt similar
procedures were applied to the
regulation of wool and milk
products, but the reviewer
has not yet come across any
comparable documents.

opened that book of the destruction which those twelve last
shepherds had wrought, and he
showed before the Lord of the
sheep that they had destroyed
even more than those before
them. And I looked until
the Lord of the sheep came to
them and took in his hand the
staff of his anger and struck
the earth; and the earth was
split; and all the animals
and the birds of heaven fell
from those sheep and sank in
the earth, and it closed over
them. And I looked until a
big sword was given to the
sheep, and the sheep went out
against all the wild animals
to kill them, and all the
animals and the birds of heaven
fled before them. *And I*
looked until a throne was
set up in the pleasant land,
and the Lord of the sheep sat
on it; and they took all the
sealed books and opened those
books before the Lord of the
sheep ...
And those seventy shepherds
were judged and found guilty,
and they also were thrown into
that abyss of fire ...
And after this those three who
were dressed in white and had
taken hold of me by my hand,
the ones who had brought me
up at first—they, with the
hand of that ram also holding
me, took me up and put me down
in the middle of those sheep
before the judgment was held.
And those sheep were all white
and their wool thick and pure.

As the above comparison indicates, numerous motifs relative to the sealed books in the Animal Apocalypse are closely paralleled in Mesopotamian herding practices. Noteworthy in this regard are the author's references to the Lord of the sheep, the undershepherds, the command to slay a limited number of sheep, the accountability of the undershepherds, and the opening of the sealed books or tablets. Even the throne on which the Lord of the sheep is seated at the opening of the books might be reminiscent of royal sheep owners mentioned by Postgate.

To sum up, Daniel 7's picture of the judgment is not only comparable to laments addressed to the shepherd judge in the Psalter, but is also closely paralleled in 1 En 90:20, where judgment takes place before the Lord of the sheep. In the latter instance, our above comparison reveals that the apocalyptic motif of the opening of the books is firmly rooted in the pastoral world of the ancient Near East. [118] On these two counts, the judge in Daniel 7 who (1) takes away the dominion of the beasts at (2) the opening of the books, is to be identified as a shepherd figure.

(9) The predator is the (destructive) SHEPHERD of the oppressed

Although the wild beasts in the psalms of lament discussed above may originally have represented adversaries of various kinds, the young lions of Ps 58:7 are identified with the unrighteous judges or "rams" of vss. 2–3:

Do you indeed decree what is right, you "rams?" Do you judge the sons of men uprightly? Nay, in your hearts you devise wrongs; your hands deal violence on earth.

Dahood and Miller are probably correct in translating ʾēlem as "leaders" or "rams," i.e., defective spelling for ʾēlîm. [119] Comparable is Ezekiel 34, which depicts Israel's oppressive shepherd judges as both rams and predators (vss. 17, 10):

As for you, my flock, thus says the Lord God: Behold, I judge between sheep and sheep, rams and he-goats.

no longer shall the shepherds feed themselves. *I will rescue my sheep from their mouths*, that they may not be food for them.

In Eze 34:10, the faithless shepherds who have given the flock as food to the wild beasts (cf. vss. 5, 8) are themselves depicted as predators (cf. Ps 22:22 "Save me from the mouth of the lion"). A parallel train of thought is displayed in 2 Targum Esther 1.2, where Pelatiah the son of Benaiah remonstrates with Nebuchadnezzar on account of his cruelty to the Jews:

He said to him: "When one delivers his flock to a shepherd, and a bear comes and snatches away a sheep, of whom will it be required?" The king answered: "From the

---

[118] Cf. also Eissfeldt (1960), who argues that 1 Sam 25:29 ("the bundle of the living") represents an earlier form of the book of the living concept found in Ps 69:29; Ex 32:32f. Eissfeldt's view is based on the study of Oppenheim (1959, 121–128), who discusses the Nuzi custom of registering sheep and goats by means of pebbles transferred to receptacles.
[119] Dahood 1968, 57; Miller 1971, 182.

shepherd will it be required." Whereupon Pelatiah rejoined: "Let thine ears hear what thy mouth has uttered." The king then ordered to bring Zedekiah before him, and he removed the iron and brass chains from him, and changed his prison garments for others.[120]

Here the oppressive gentile ruler is depicted as both negligent undershepherd and destructive predator. A similar logic possibly informs other OT passages describing shepherd rulers and judges as wild beasts. By depriving the oppressed of their legal rights, these have become enemies rather than defenders of the flock. Thus the shepherds are referred to as ravenous dogs (Isa 56:11), as roaring lions and ravenous wolves (Zeph 3:3 cf. v. 13), while the wicked ruler of the poor is described as a roaring lion or a charging bear (Prov 28:15). Similarly, immediately preceding Zechariah's allegory of the worthless shepherd (11:4f.), shepherds and lions are used in parallelism (v. 3). Finally, in Hos 13:5–8, Yahweh the shepherd of Israel turns against his flock and becomes as a lion, a panther and a bear:

It was I who knew you in the wilderness, in the land of drought; but when they had fed to the full (*kmr*^{c}*ytm*), they were filled, and their heart was lifted up; therefore they forgot me. So I will be to them like a lion, like a leopard I will lurk beside the way. I will fall upon them like a bear robbed of her cubs, I will tear open their breast, and there I will devour them like a lion, as a wild beast would rend them.

It might, therefore, be reasonably supposed that in the exilic/post-exilic period, the wild beasts in Israel's psalms of lament not only served to represent the nation's foreign rulers, but also described them in their capacity as oppressive shepherds. The same should be said of the predators representing the gentile kings of Daniel 7. As noted above, the horned beasts of Daniel 7 and 8 represent gentile rulers as herd leaders or shepherds, and reference to Yahweh the shepherd as a lion, panther and bear in Hos 13:5–8 raises the possibility that the first three beasts of Daniel 7 likewise symbolize oppressive shepherd rulers. Moreover, the beasts of Daniel 7 are judged at the opening of the books in a passage strikingly similar to 1 En 90:20 (see above). As we have already observed, however, such books in the Animal Apocalypse and in Mesopotamian herding culture serve the practical purpose of assessing the faithfulness of undershepherds entrusted with the care of the flock. In view of these considerations, it is probable that the predators judged from the books in Daniel 7 are to be identified as Israel's gentile undershepherds. That such are depicted as physical anomalies is consistent with the use made of birth omens to describe shepherd rulers in Mesopotamian, Jewish apocalyptic and Christian apocalyptic texts, which have already been noted above.

---

[120] Ginzberg 1909–55, 6:383 (n. 8).

(10) The man is the SHEPHERD of the animals

The man-beast contrast in Daniel 7 is most pronounced in vss. 4, 12–14. In v. 4, the lion "was made to stand upon two feet like a man; and the mind of a man was given to it," while in vss. 12–14, the dominion forfeited by the beasts in the judgment is given to one like a son of man. In both instances, the human image derives from the ancient Near Eastern and OT notion of the universal shepherd king who rules over the beasts of the nations.

a. *Universal shepherd ruler—Mesopotamian texts.* Claims to a universal shepherd rule appear already in a self-laudatory hymn to Šulgi (ca. 2046–1998 BCE):

King of the four corners (of the universe) am I,
Herdsman, shepherd of the blackheads am I[121]

Again, in the *Deification of Lipit-Ishtar* (ca. 1870 BCE), the shepherd king rules the foreign nations with the yoke:

The black-headed people—driven like sheep—shall go in their yoke the straight (path) for thee, O Lipit-Ishtar, the foreign countries—thou shalt be their king, far (and wide).[122]

Of particular interest, however, is a text ascribed to Aššur-naṣir-pal II (884–859 BCE), in which shepherd terminology serves the ruler's claims to a universal dominion involving wild and domestic animals, men and lands:

(5) *... the wonderful shepherd who fears no battle,* ... (7) *who has conquered all mankind* .... (85) *Ninurta and Palil, who love my priesthood, (86) bestowed on me the beasts of the field* and called me to go hunting. (86—sic) I slew 450 mighty lions, and 390 wild bulls I slew (87) with my .... chariots (88) (and) by my lordly onslaught, I cut (down) (89) 200 ostriches like caged birds and (90) 30 elephants (91) I cast into the pit. 50 live wild bulls, (92) 140 live ostriches, (93) 20 mighty lions with my weapon (94) and my .... I captured. (95) 5 live wild elephants from the governor of (96) Suḫi and the governor of Lubda I received, (97) they went along with me on my march. *Of bulls, lions and ostriches, apes male and female, I collected their herds (100) and caused them to bring forth their increase. To the land of Assyria (more) land, and to its people (more) people for .... I added.*[123]

According to this text, beasts and nations alike are subject to the Assyrian shepherd conqueror, and are added to his herds. That the king's hunting activities (line 86) also serve this concept is indicated by comparison with an earlier text from Tiglath-pileser I (1112–1074 BCE):

Herds of gazelles, stags, ibex, antelopes,—since Aššur and Adad, the gods who love

---

[121] Pritchard (ed.) 1969, 584.
[122] Frankfort 1978, 298.
[123] Wiseman 1952, 29, 31.

me, have given me the practice of hunting,—they allowed me to hunt on lofty forest mountains. I assembled herds and counted their number as a shepherd counts his sheep.[124]

b. *Universal shepherd ruler—OT and apocalyptic texts*. Comparable to the Aššur-naṣir-pal text are Jer 27:2, 5–7 and Jer 28:14, where the captive nations wear the yoke of Nebuchadnezzar, who rules men and beasts alike:

Thus the Lord said to me: Make yourself *thongs and yoke-bars*, and put them on your neck.

It is I who by my great power and my outstretched arm have made the earth, with the men and animals that are on the earth, and I give it to whomever it seems right to me. Now I have given *all these lands* into the hand of Nebuchadnezzar, the king of Babylon, my servant, and *I have given him also the beasts of the field to serve him. All the nations shall serve him* ...

I have put upon the neck of all these nations an iron yoke of servitude to Nebuchadnezzar king of Babylon, and *they shall serve him, for I have given to him even the beasts of the field.*

Just as Aššur-naṣir-pal includes the subject lands among his herds since Ninurta and Palil have bestowed on him the beasts of the field, so in Jeremiah 27 and 28, the nations wear Nebuchadnezzar's yoke because Yahweh has given to him even the beasts of the field. That the yoke worn by Nebuchadnezzar's subjects points to his shepherd office is further indicated by comparison with Ezekiel 34: in the Jeremiah narrative, Hananiah breaks Jeremiah's yoke-bars (Jer 28:10–11), while in Ezekiel 34, Yahweh breaks the yoke-bars of his captive *flock* (v. 27):

And they [the flock] shall know that I am the Lord, when I break the bars of their yoke, and deliver them from the hand of those who enslaved them.[124a]

Turning to the book of Daniel, we find reference to Nebuchadnezzar's universal sovereignty over men and beasts in both chapters 2 and 4. Dan 2:37–38 probably alludes to the Jeremiah passages discussed above:

You, O king, the king of kings, to whom the God of heaven has given the kingdom, the power, and the might, and the glory, and into whose hand he has given, wherever they dwell, *the sons of men, the beasts of the field, and the birds of the air, making you rule over them all*—you are the head of gold.

Similarly, Daniel 4 depicts the king of Babylon as a world tree, whose dominion extends over the beasts of the field and the birds of the air (vss. 17–19):

---

[124] Schrader 1889–1915, 1, Prisma-Inschrift Col. 7 (lines 4–12).
[124a] Cf. n. 122 above.

The tree you saw, which grew and became strong, so that its top reached to heaven, and it was visible to the end of the whole earth; whose leaves were fair and its fruit abundant, and in which was food for all; *under which beasts of the field found shade, and in whose branches the birds of the air dwelt* — it is you, O king, who have grown and become strong. Your greatness has grown and reaches to heaven, and *your dominion to the ends of the earth.*

Inclusion of the tree metaphor in this context is instructive, since, as Moortgat,[125] Seibert[126] and Genge[127] have shown, the "tree of life" or "sacral tree" in Mesopotamian culture symbolizes the shepherd, who both feeds and rules over his flock. Such is certainly the function of Nebuchadnezzar's tree in Daniel 4, and it is against such a background that the imagery of the chapter is most readily understood: when the universal shepherd loses his throne, the tree is cut down and the king banished to a beast-like existence comparable to that of the subject nations (cf. *ḥywt br'*, vss. 18, 22).[128] Such a background might then be supposed for Dan 5:18–21, where Nebuchadnezzar loses his human status when he ceases to function as divinely appointed world ruler:

O king, the Most High God gave Nebuchadnezzar your father kingship and greatness and glory and majesty; and because of the greatness that he gave him, all peoples, nations, and languages trembled and feared before him; whom he would he slew, and whom he would he kept alive; whom he would he raised up, and whom he would he put down. But when his heart was lifted up and his spirit was hardened so that he dealt proudly, *he was deposed from his kingly throne*, and his glory was taken from him; he was driven from among men, *and his mind was made like that of a beast.*

The human as opposed to beast-like status of the world shepherd in Daniel 4 and 5 provides an important clue to the lion and son of man images in chapter 7. The fact that Babylon the lion is the most "human" of the four beasts corresponds to the position of honour accorded the king of Babylon as world ruler in chapters 2, 4 and 5,[129] while the son of man's enthronement as universal sovereign coincides with the subjection of the beasts of the nations in the judgment. In fact, the same powers ascribed to the king of Babylon in Jer 27:6–7, Dan 2:37–38 and 5:18–19 are those which are given to the son of man in these verses:[130]

---

[125] Moortgat 1949, 27–32, 103, 106 etc.
[126] Seibert 1969, 35–37.
[127] Genge 1971, 321–334.
[128] Cf. the following (contemptuous?) reference to the conquered population of Sumer (?): "Like sheep they eat grass with their mouths, water out of the garden beds they drink" (Falkenstein 1950, 128).
[129] Cf. Koch 1961, 15.
[130] Cf. Herzfeld 1947, 2:833.

Jer 27:6–7

and I have given him also the
beasts of the field to serve
him.
All the nations shall serve
him.

Dan 7:12–14

As for the rest of the beasts,
their dominion was taken away ...
there came one like a son of man ...
And to him was given dominion
and glory and kingdom, that all
peoples, nations, and languages
should serve him ...

Dan 2:37–38

You, O king, the king of kings,
to whom the God of heaven has
given the kingdom, the power,
and the might, and the glory,
and into whose hand he has given,
wherever they dwell, the sons of
men, the beasts of the field, and
the birds of the air, making you
rule over them all ...

Dan 5:18–19

O king, the Most High God gave
Nebuchadnezzar your father kingship and greatness and glory and
majesty;
and because of the greatness that
he gave him, all peoples, nations
and languages trembled and feared
before him ...

Just as Nebuchadnezzar's universal rule is described in terms of his divinely
appointed sovereignty over the animal world, so world dominion is granted
to the son of man when the beasts of the nations are judged by the Ancient of
Days.[131]

Also comparable to Dan 7:12–14 are Gen 1:26; Ps 8:5–9 and Ps 80:9–14,
18, where universal dominion is described in terms of man's relation to the
animal world:

Then God said, Let us make *man* in our image, after our likeness, and let them have
*dominion over the fish of the sea, and over the birds of the air, and over the cattle,
and over all the earth, and over every creeping thing that creeps upon the earth.*

what is man that thou art mindful of him, and *the son of man* that thou dost care for
him? Yet thou hast made him little less than God, and dost *crown him with glory and
honour*, Thou hast given him *dominion* over the works of thy hands; *thou hast put all*

---

[131] Cf. 1 En 90:33, where the predators are included in the Lord of the sheep's flock at the
end-time.

things under his feet, all sheep and oxen, and also the beasts of the field, the birds of the air, and the fish of the sea, whatever passes along the paths of the sea.

Thou didst bring a vine out of Egypt; thou didst drive out the nations and plant it. Thou didst clear the ground for it; *it* took deep root and *filled the land. The mountains were covered with its shade, the "cedars of El" with its branches; it sent out its branches to the sea, and its shoots to the River.* Why then hast thou broken down its walls, so that all who pass along the way pluck its fruit? The *boar* from the forest ravages it, and *all that move in the field feed on it.*

But let thy hand be upon *the man* of thy right hand, *the son of man* whom thou hast made strong for thyself!

In each of the above passages, royal imagery is applied to a "man" or a "son of man" whose sovereignty is viewed in terms of his relation to the animal kingdom. Like the king of Babylon, he rules over the beasts of the field and the birds of the air (Gen 1:26; Ps 8:8–9), he receives "glory," "honour" and "dominion" (Ps 8:6–7 cf. Gen 1:26), while in Psalm 80, he is depicted as a cosmic vine comparable to Nebuchadnezzar's world tree in Daniel 4.[132]

In the case of Psalm 80, it should also be noted that this lament for the cosmic vine/son of man is addressed to the heavenly shepherd of Israel (v. 2), which raises the possibility that the vine of his planting represents his earthly counterpart as universal shepherd. Reference to the "cedars of El" covered by the shade of the vine in v. 11 lends support to this view, since these are comparable to the rival cedars in Lebanon, the garden of God (Eze 31:8), which are overshadowed by the world tree representing the king of Egypt (vss. 5–6). Since Lebanon's cedars are referred to as "shepherds" in Zech 11:1–3 (cf. Jer 25:34–38), it might be said that the cedars covered by the cosmic vine or cosmic tree in Psalm 80 and Ezekiel 31 are rival shepherd rulers overshadowed by the kings of Israel and Egypt respectively. Such being the case, the son of man in Psalm 80 is to be identified as a universal shepherd, whose dominion is disputed by the gentile nations, "the boar from the forest ... and all that move in the field" (v. 14).

To sum up, the man-beast contrast observed in connection with the man-like lion and the son of man in Daniel 7 reflects the notion of the universal shepherd king who rules over the beasts of the nations. Both figures are reminiscent of passages describing Nebuchadnezzar as universal

---

[132] Cf. Zimmerli 1969, 328: "Am ungebrochensten ist diese fromme Bildsprache in Ps 80:9ff. zu erkennen, wo Israel als der aus Ägypten verpflanzte edle Weinstock, der sich unversehens zum Weltenbaum auswächst, geschildert wird." Similarly, Stolz 1972, 144: "In Ps 80:11 werden die Zedern Els *ʾarzê ʾel* genannt; die Zedern sind ja das Libanon-Gewächs kat'exochen. In v. 10ff. ist überhaupt die Vorstellung, ähnlich wie in Eze 31, die, dass der Weltenbaum, mit dem Israel verglichen wird, die Els-Zedern, also die übrigen Bäume des Gottesgartens, überragt."

shepherd in Jeremiah 27–28 and Daniel 2, 4 and 5, while the title "son of man" in Daniel 7:13 is also comparable to Gen 1:26, Psalm 8 and Psalm 80, where, as in the case of Nebuchadnezzar, universal dominion is again viewed in terms of sovereignty over the animal world.

Since Psalm 80 identifies the son of man with the community (80:9 cf. Dan 7:14, 27), whose foes are depicted as rebellious beasts (80:14 cf. Daniel 7) opposed by a heavenly being enthroned on the storm (80:2 cf. Dan 7:13),[133] it is probable that the author of Daniel 7 drew the term "son of man" from this communal lament.

(11) The storm god is the SHEPHERD of the flock

In Daniel 7, the four beasts from the sea lose their dominion to the cloud-riding son of man (vss. 3, 12–14, 26). Scholars have long recognized elements of traditional *Chaoskampf* imagery in these verses. In the Babylonian poem *Enuma eliš*, for example, Marduk rides the storm chariot in battle against Tiamat and the monsters from the deep, while in Canaanite mythology, Baal, the rider of the clouds, vanquishes the sea monster Yamm. Similarly, in the OT, various chaos monsters are destroyed by Yahweh (Ps 89:9–11; 74:13–17; Isa 27:1; 51:9–10).

Recourse to such parallels has so far failed to account for the actual beasts described in Daniel 7, nearly all of which are conspicuously absent in the chaos myths traditionally cited.

As argued above, however, these animals represent the enemies of Israel the flock, and it is noteworthy that in both *Enuma eliš* and the OT, the storm god who conquers the sea is depicted as a shepherd:[134]

---

[133] Cf. n. 137 below.

[134] Less certain is the identification of Yamm's adversary as a shepherd in the Canaanite texts. However, cf. Cross (1973, 147–148), who proposes the following restoration of RS 24.245 (lines 1–3):

bʿl. yṯb. kṯbt. ǵr.	Baʿl sits enthroned, (his) mountain like a dais,
hd. r[ʿy] (2) k mdb.	Haddu the shepherd, like the Flood dragon,
btk. ǵrh. ʾil ṣpn.	In the midst of his mount, Divine Ṣapōn,
b[m] (3) ǵr. tlʾiyt.	On the mount of (his) victory.

According to Cross, the above text refers to the return of Baal "from victory over Yamm or the flood-dragon, and his subsequent sitting in state on his throne, manifesting himself as lord of the storm" (p. 148). The reading *hd. r* [ʿy] ("Haddu the she[pherd]") follows Virolleaud's restoration in *Ugaritica V* and has also been accepted by Fisher and Knutson (1969, 157–158). Perhaps comparable is the expression *hd. rʿy* in RS 24.252.

In the Ugaritic text III AB A, Baal employs the two clubs *ygrš* and *ʾymr* to smite his adversary Yamm. Ginsberg (1935, 328) compares these two clubs with the shepherd's two staffs *nʿm* and *ḥblym* in Zech 11:7f.

a. *Enuma eliš*. In Tablet VII of *Enuma eliš*, Tiamat's conqueror is twice referred to as a shepherd (lines 70–75; 124–132):

SIR.SIR, who heaped up a mountain over her, Tiamat,
Who the corpse of Tiamat carried off with his weapon;
Who directs the land—their faithful *shepherd*;
Whose ... means cultivation, whose spear means furrows;
Who the wide-spreading Tiamat vaulted in his wrath,
Crossing (her) like a bridge at the place of single combat.

NEBIRU shall hold the crossings of heaven and earth;
Those who failed of crossing above and below;
   Ever of him shall inquire.
Nebiru is the star which in the skies is brilliant.
Verily, he governs their turnings, to him indeed they look,
Saying: "He who the midst of the Sea restlessly crosses,
Let 'Crossing' be his name who controls its midst.
May they uphold the course of the stars of heaven;
May he shepherd all the gods like sheep.
May he vanquish Tiamat; may her life be strait and short!"

b. *OT texts*. In the following passages, Israel's shepherd God is depicted as the storm or the conqueror of the sea: Ex 15:8, 10, 13; Ps 77:17–21; 68:5, 8–11, 23, 34; 74:1, 13–14; 78:52–53; 80:2; Isa 63:11–14; Zech 9:14, 16; 10:1–3, 11.

Ex 15:8, 10, 13
At the blast of thy nostrils the waters piled up,
the floods stood up in a heap;
the deeps congealed in the heart of the sea.

Thou didst blow with thy wind, the sea covered them;
they sank as lead in the mighty waters.

Thou hast led in thy steadfast love the people whom thou hast
redeemed, thou has guided them by thy strength to thy holy abode.

Although the sea in Exodus 15 is a passive instrument in Yahweh's battle against the Egyptians, allusions to the storm in vss. 8 and 10 unmistakably allude to the primeval battle between the divine warrior and the inimical sea. Verse 13 depicts the divine shepherd, who leads (*nḥh*) his flock to their abode (*nwh*) (cf. Ps 77:21, discussed below).

Ps 77:17–21
When the waters saw thee, O God,
when the waters saw thee, they were afraid,
yea, the deep trembled.
The clouds poured out water;
the skies gave forth thunder;
thy arrows flashed on every side.
The crash of thy thunder was in the whirlwind;

thy lightnings lighted up the world;
the earth trembled and shook.
Thy way was through the sea,
thy path through the great waters;
yet thy footprints were unseen.
Thou didst lead thy people like a flock
by the hand of Moses and Aaron.

Here the storm God triumphantly leads his flock through the vanquished sea. As in Ex 15:13, *nḥh* (v. 21) describes the action of the divine shepherd. Although some commentators feel that v. 21 was added by an editor, it has excellent continuity both with v. 16 and with vss. 17–20.

Ps 68:5, 8–11, 23, 34
Sing to God, sing praises to his name; lift up a song to him who rides upon the clouds; his name is the Lord, exult before him!

O God, when thou didst go forth before thy people, when thou didst march through the wilderness, the earth quaked, the heavens poured down rain, at the presence of God; yon Sinai quaked at the presence of God, the God of Israel. Rain in abundance, O God, thou didst shed abroad; thou didst restore thy heritage as it languished; thy flock found a dwelling in it; in thy goodness, O God, thou didst provide for the needy.

The Lord said, "I will bring them back from Bashan, I will bring them back from the depths of the sea"

to him who rides in the heavens, the ancient heavens; lo, he sends forth his voice, his mighty voice.

In this ancient and notoriously difficult psalm, Elohim is referred to as *rkb bᶜrbwt* (v. 5), which many scholars regard as a corruption of *rkb ᶜrpt*, ("Cloud Rider"), one of the stock epithets of Baal in the Ugaritic literature. V. 34 is reminiscent of the Ugaritic text II AB V 70, where the expression *ytn qlh* is used of Baal when he thunders. Reference to Elohim as a raingiver in Ps 68:10 agrees with this idea, while the myth of the dragon fight is alluded to in v. 23.[135] Vss. 8 and 11 indicate that the storm God is a shepherd. The expression *yṣ lpny* (v. 8) describes the action of the shepherd who goes before his flock (cf. Num 27:17),[136] and it is probable that Israel the flock is referred to in v. 11 (*ḥyh*).

Ps 74:1, 13–14
O God, why dost thou cast us off for ever? Why dost thy anger smoke against the sheep of thy pasture?

Thou didst divide the sea by thy might; thou didst break the heads of the dragons on

---
[135] Cf. Hammershaimb 1960, 88–89.
[136] J. Jeremias 1968, 487 n. 19.

the waters. Thou didst crush the heads of Leviathan, thou didst give him as food for the creatures of the wilderness.

According to these verses, the monsters of chaos are vanquished by Israel's shepherd God.

Ps 78:52–53

The motif of the shepherd's victory over the sea is also alluded to in Ps 78:52–53:

Then he led forth his people like sheep, and guided them in the wilderness like a flock. He led them in safety, so that they were not afraid; but the sea overwhelmed their enemies.

Ps 80:2

Give ear, O Shepherd of Israel, thou who leadest Joseph like a flock! Thou who art enthroned upon the cherubim, shine forth

This verse depicts the Shepherd of Israel as a storm deity, comparable to the Canaanite Baal:

Die Vorstellung von dem auf den Keruben thronenden Gott ist ursprünglich kanaanäisch, sie bezieht sich auf den über den Wolken thronenden Himmelsherrn (vgl. zu *rkb ⁽rpt* in Ps 68:5). Der in Silo verehrte *yhwh ṣbᵓwt* wurde in Israel zuerst als "der über den Keruben Thronende" bezeichnet (vgl. 1 S 4, 4). Diese Vorstellung ging dann aber mit der Lade nach Jerusalem über (2 S 6, 2) und ist in der Kulttradition des Zion festzustellen (Ps 18, 11; 97, 2; 99,1). Wie der Himmelsbaal als Gewittergottheit "aufstrahlte", so soll nun Jahwe als Kerubenthroner "erscheinen".[137]

Isa 63:11–14

Then he remembered the days of old, of Moses his servant. Where is he who brought up out of the sea the shepherds of his flock? Where is he who put in the midst of them his holy Spirit, who caused his glorious arm to go at the right hand of Moses, who divided the waters before them to make for himself an everlasting name, who led them through the depths? Like a horse in the desert, they did not stumble. Like cattle that go down into the valley, the Spirit of the Lord gave them rest. So thou didst lead thy people, to make for thyself a glorious name.

Here Israel's shepherd God who led his flock through the sea is called upon to deliver his people from their immediate distress.

Zech 9:14, 16; 10:1–3, 11

Then the Lord will appear over them, and his arrow go forth like lightning; the Lord God will sound the trumpet, and march forth in the whirlwinds of the south.

On that day the Lord their God will save them for they are the flock of his people; for like jewels of a crown they shall shine on his land.

---

[137] Kraus 1972, 557.

Ask rain from the Lord in the season of the spring rain, from the Lord who makes the storm clouds, who gives men showers of rain, to every one the vegetation in the field. For the teraphim utter nonsense, and the diviners see lies; the dreamers tell false dreams, and give empty consolation. Therefore the people wander like sheep; they are afflicted for want of a shepherd. My anger is hot against the shepherds, and I will punish the leaders; for the Lord of hosts cares for his flock, the house of Judah, and will make them like his proud steed in battle.

They shall pass through the sea of Egypt, and the waves of the sea shall be smitten, and all the depths of the Nile dried up.

As Hanson has already noted,[138] the *Chaoskampf* myth underlies the imagery of these verses, which describe the eschatological victory of Yahweh's flock.

In several of the OT passages we have reviewed, the recollection of Yahweh's deliverance of his flock at the sea of Egypt undergirds the hope of a future salvation for his lamenting worshippers (Psalms 74; 77; Isa 63:7–64:11). Of particular interest in this regard are Psalm 74 and Isa 63:7–64:11, with their references to Israel's desolate temple (Ps 74:3–4; Isa 63:18; 64:11). Such passages may well have spoken with renewed force to Maccabean Israel, and revived the hope that the God who delivered his flock from the sea might yet deliver Israel from gentile invaders again defiling her house of worship. In Psalm 74, Israel calls on Yahweh who crushed Leviathan to deliver his flock in judgment from the wild beasts (vss. 4, 19), and in a similar manner, perhaps, Daniel 7 awaits deliverance from the beasts of the nations, who are shortly to forfeit their dominion to the cloud-riding son of man.

(12) God is the SHEPHERD of Israel

As already argued above, the one who judges from the books (Dan 7:10) and restores the sanctuary (Dan 8:14) is a shepherd figure. The title "shepherd" is used of Yahweh in Gen 48:15; 49:24, Ps 23:1 and in the communal lament Psalm 80 (v. 2), while shepherd vocabulary describing the God of Israel appears in numerous other laments (e.g., Psalms 44, 74, 77, 79, Isa 63:7–64:11).

External metaphor interaction in Daniel 7 and 8

In Chapter Three, we proposed an interpretative model for the animal metaphors of Daniel 7 and 8 and their various functional characteristics. It was suggested that a root metaphor taken from the world of predators and

---

[138] Hanson 1975, 322, 332.

horned beasts has generated new external metaphors in each of the eleven domains relative to the animals of these chapters. We also proposed that these external metaphors have in turn established internal relationships within their respective domains, and then, by interacting across these domains, produced the functional hybrids described in both chapters. An analogous example, we argued, was to be found in the cases of interaction occurring among the external metaphors describing the various ordered hierarchies of Medieval-Elizabethan Britain, which may be illustrated schematically in the following way:

(a) The king   is the CHIEF of   (b) the State
(c) The sun   is the CHIEF of   (d) the planets
(e) The lion   is the CHIEF of   (f) the animals
(g) The head   is the CHIEF of   (h) the body

Here the root metaphor "chief" provides the basis for four external metaphors, which then interact across their respective domains as follows: "The sun is the royal planet" (c–a–d); "The king is the sun of the State" (a–c–b); "The lion-hearted king" (e–a); "The king is the head of the body politic" (a–g–h–b); "The lion-hearted king shines over the body politic" (e–a–c–h–b).

It is our argument that, in a similar fashion, the root metaphor "shepherd" has generated the following external metaphors informing Daniel 7 and 8:

(a) The herd leader   is the SHEPHERD of   (b) the flock
(c) The military leader is the SHEPHERD of   (d) the warriors
(e) The warrior   is the (destructive)
                         SHEPHERD of   (f) the enemy
(g) The ruler   is the SHEPHERD of   (h) the nation
(i) God/Michael   is the SHEPHERD of   (j) the angels
(k) The ruler   is the SHEPHERD of   (l) the temple
(m) God   is the SHEPHERD of   (n) truth
(o) The judge   is the SHEPHERD of   (p) the oppressed
(q) The predator   is the (destructive)
                         SHEPHERD of   (r) the oppressed
(s) The man   is the SHEPHERD of   (t) the animals
(u) The storm god   is the SHEPHERD of   (v) the flock
(w) God   is the SHEPHERD of   (x) Israel

The functional peculiarities of the animals in Daniel 7 and 8 can now be described according to the following interactions: "The predators are enemies of the storm god" (q–e–u); "The ten-horned beast makes war on the saints" (a–e–j); "God judges the predators and the ten-horned beast" (w–o–q/a); "The son of man rules over the beasts of the nations" (s–k–q–g); "The lion becomes a man" (q–s); "The he-goat attacks the ram" (a–e–a);

"The he-goat rises up against the Prince" (a–e–i); "God the judge vindicates the downtrodden temple" (w–o–p–l); "The beasts are rulers" (q/a–k).

Conclusion

In this chapter, we noted that Daniel 7 and 8, along with chapters 9–12, lament the continuation of Israel's bondage to Antiochus, here viewed as the nation's final gentile oppressor of the "exilic" era. In view of this, we turned to OT lamentation texts sharing Daniel 7–12's eschatological orientation *vis-à-vis* the restoration for antecedents to the animal metaphors of chapters 7 and 8. Examination of such antecedents led us to the conclusion that the root metaphor "shepherd" informs the various semantic domains relative to the beasts of these chapters. Each of the twelve external metaphors discussed brought to view a particular aspect of the office of the shepherd ruler or his heavenly counterpart, and it was also noted that in Mesopotamian, Jewish apocalyptic and Christian apocalyptic texts, shepherd gods and shepherd kings are depicted as animal anomalies of the type already discussed in Part II of this study. Finally, we proposed that interactions across the various domains in Daniel 7 and 8 account for the functional peculiarities of the animals described in these two chapters.

Concluding remarks

Every age has its prevailing metaphors which impress people at the time as having unusual power and meaning. In the West, images such as the prison, the wasteland, the monster, the machine and the hospital have frequently described the present human condition.[1] In the tumultuous years marked by Antiochus' campaign against Hebrew worship, Israel's self-understanding was profoundly influenced by the image of the shepherd. As indicated in this study, both the author of the Animal Apocalypse and the author of the Daniel visions considered it highly appropriate to summon Israel's resistance to foreign rule by means of the shepherd metaphor.

For the author of the Daniel visions, the shepherd metaphor was a powerful reminder of the God repeatedly addressed in the laments of Israel in "exile." Once again, the gentiles were in the land, defiling the temple and destroying the people of the covenant, and instinctively, perhaps, the author turned to laments of an earlier age to express the anguish and hopes of his own generation. In old complaints which awaited eschatological deliverance from the gentile beasts attacking temple and flock, he heard a prophetic note addressed to his, the last generation of the "exile," just as the Qumran and NT communities were to find in various psalms direct predictions of their own day.

Our author, moreover, also shared a marked interest in Mesopotamian birth-omen traditions which from earliest times gave rise to vivid animal metaphors describing shepherd gods and shepherd kings. It is this cosmopolitan element in Daniel—already intimated in the narrative section of the book—which accounts for the author's bizarre animal anomalies in chapters 7 and 8.

The evidence reviewed in this study indicates that it was the office of the king, as witnessed in Israel and Mesopotamia, which mediated the shepherd metaphor to the various domains relative to the beasts of Daniel 7 and 8. In his capacity as shepherd, the king was a man of omen (in Mesopotamia and apocalyptic), who functioned as herd leader, warrior, ruler, temple builder, guardian of truth, judge, devourer of enemy flocks and universal ruler of beasts and lands alike. Projection of the king's office on to the heavenly realm made room for the notion of a divine shepherd who led the stars in battle, revealed himself in the storm, and graciously answered the complaints of his afflicted worshippers, even in Maccabean times.

---

[1] Embler 1967, 368–382.

Bibliography

Armstrong, John. 1981. *The Idea of Holiness and the Humane Response*. London.

Barfield, A. O. 1947. "Poetic Diction and Legal Fiction." In *Essays Presented to Charles Williams*. Introduction by C. S. Lewis. London. 106–127.

— 1960. "The Meaning of the Word 'Literal.'" In *Metaphor and Symbol*. Edited by L. C. Knights and Basil Cottle. London. 48–63.

Barton, George A. 1929. *The Royal Inscriptions of Sumer and Akkad*. New Haven.

Bauckham, Richard J. 1978. "The Rise of Apocalyptic." *Themelios* 3/2:10–23.

Beale, Gregory K. 1980. "The Danielic Background for Relevation 13:18 and 17:9." *Tyndale Bulletin* 31: 163–170.

Becker, Joachim. 1966. *Israel deutet seine Psalmen*. Stuttgarter Bibelstudien 18. Stuttgart.

Becker, Jürgen. 1970. *Untersuchungen zur Entstehungsgeschichte der Testamente der zwölf Patriarchen*. Leiden.

Beekman, J., and Callow, J. 1974. *Translating the Word of God*. Grand Rapids.

Beer, Georg. 1900. "Das Buch Henoch." In *Die Apokryphen und Pseudepigraphen des Alten Testaments*. Edited by E. Kautzsch. Vol. 2. Tübingen. 217–310.

Behrmann, Georg. 1894. *Das Buch Daniel*. Handkommentar zum Alten Testament. Göttingen.

Bentzen, Aage. 1952. *Daniel*. Handbuch zum Alten Testament 19. Tübingen.

Beyerlin, Walter, ed. 1978. *Near Eastern Religious Texts Relating to the Old Testament*. Philadelphia.

Black, Max. 1962. *Models and Metaphors*. Ithaca, New York.

— 1979. "More About Metaphor." In *Metaphor and Thought*. Edited by Andrew Ortony. Cambridge. 19–43.

Booth, Wayne C. 1978. "Metaphor as Rhetoric: The Problem of Evaluation." *Critical Inquiry* 5: 49–72.

Borger, R. 1971. "Gott Marduk und Gott-König Šulgi als Propheten. Zwei prophetische Texte." *Bibliotheca Orientalis* 28 :3–21.

Breasted, James H. 1906–1907. *Ancient Records of Egypt: the Historical Documents*. 5 vols. Chicago.

— 1912. *Development of Religion and Thought in Ancient Egypt*. London.

Büchler, A. 1967. *Studies in Sin and Atonement in the Rabbinic Literature of the First Century*. New York.

Buttrick, George Arthur, ed. 1962. *Interpreter's Dictionary of the Bible*. 4 vols. Nashville and New York.

Caquot, André. 1955. "Sur les quatre bêtes de Daniel VII." *Semitica* 5: 5–13.

— 1967. "Les quatre bêtes et le 'Fils d'homme' (Daniel 7)." *Semitica* 17: 37–71.

Casey, Maurice. 1979. *Son of Man*. London.

Castellino, G. R. 1972. *Two Šulgi Hymns (BC)*. Studi Semitici 42. Rome.

Charles, R. H., ed. *The Apocrypha and Pseudepigrapha of the Old Testament in English*. 2 vols. Oxford. 1913.

Childs, Brevard S. 1979. *Introduction to the Old Testament as Scripture*. Philadelphia.

Cohen, M. E. 1972. "An Analysis of the Balag-Compositions to the God Enlil Copied in Babylon During the Seleucid Period." Ph.D. dissertation. University of Pennsylvania.

Collins, Adela Yarbro. 1976. *The Combat Myth in the Book of Revelation*. Missoula, Montana.

Collins, John J. 1974a. "The Symbolism of Transcendence in Jewish Apocalyptic." *Biblical*

Research. Journal of the Chicago Society of Biblical Research 19: 5–22.

— 1974b. "The Son of Man and the Saints of the Most High in the Book of Daniel." *Journal of Biblical Literature* 93: 50–66.

— 1975. "The Court-Tales in Daniel and the Development of Apocalyptic." *Journal of Biblical Literature* 94: 218–234.

— 1977. *The Apocalyptic Vision of the Book of Daniel*. Harvard Semitic Monographs 16. Missoula, Montana.

— 1981. "Apocalyptic Genre and Mythic Allusions in Daniel." *Journal for the Study of the Old Testament* 21: 83–100.

Cross, Frank Moore. 1973. *Canaanite Myth and Hebrew Epic*: Essays in the History and Religion of Israel. Cambridge, Mass.

Crossan, J. D. 1973. *In Parables*: The Challenge of the Historical Jesus. New York.

Cumont, Franz. 1909. "La plus ancienne géographie astrologique." *Klio* 9: 263–273.

Dahood, Mitchell. 1968. *Psalms 2*. Anchor Bible. Garden City, New York.

Danby, Herbert. 1933. *The Mishnah*. London.

Davies, Philip R. 1980. "Eschatology in the Book of Daniel." *Journal for the Study of the Old Testament* 17: 33–53.

Delcor, M. 1968. "Les Sources du Chapitre 7 de Daniel." *Vetus Testamentum* 18: 290–312.

— 1971. *Le livre de Daniel*. Paris.

Dennefeld, Ludwig. 1914. *Babylonisch-Assyrische Geburts-Omina*. Leipzig.

Dexinger, Ferdinand. 1969. *Das Buch Daniel und seine Probleme*. Stuttgarter Bibelstudien 36. Stuttgart.

Dijk, J. van. 1971. "Sumerische Religion." *Handbuch der Religionsgeschichte* 1: 431–496.

Dove, W. F. 1936. "Artificial Production of the Fabulous Unicorn." *Scientific Monthly* 42: 431–436.

Dunand, R. 1977. "L'oracle du potier et la formation de l'apocalyptique en Égypte." In *L'apocalyptique*. F. Raphaël et al. Paris. 50–54.

Ehrlich, Arnold B. 1914. *Randglossen zur hebräischen Bibel 7*. Leipzig.

Eissfeldt, Otto. 1960. *Der Beutel der Lebendigen. Alttestamentliche Erzählungs- und Dichtungsmotive im Lichte neuer Nuzi-texte*. Berichte über die Verhandlungen der Sächsischen Akademie der Wissenschaft zu Leipzig. Philologisch-historische Klasse, Band 105. Heft 6. Berlin.

— 1974. *The Old Testament*. Translated by Peter R. Ackroyd. Oxford.

Embler, Weller. 1967. "Five Metaphors from the Modern Repertory." In *The World of Words*: A Language Reader. Edited by Barnet Kottler and Martin Light. Boston. 368–382.

Engnell, Ivan. 1967. *Studies in Divine Kingship in the Ancient Near East*. 2nd. ed. Oxford.

Erling, B. 1972. "Ezekiel 38–39 and the Origins of Apocalyptic." In *Ex Orbe Religionum. Studia Geo Widengren*. Leiden. 104–114.

Falkenstein, A. 1944. "Untersuchungen zur sumerischen Grammatik." *Zeitschrift für Assyriologie* (Neue Folge) 14: 69–118.

— 1950. "Sumerische religiöse Texte 1. Drei Hymnen auf Ur-Ninurta von Isin." *Zeitschrift für Assyriologie* (Neue Folge) 15: 80–150.

— and Soden, W. von. 1953. *Sumerische und Akkadische Hymnen und Gebete*. Zürich and Stuttgart.

Farrer, Austin M. 1951. *A Study in St. Mark*. London.

Finkelstein, J. J. 1963. "Mesopotamian Historiography." In *Cuneiform Studies and the History of Civilization*. Proceedings of the American Philosophical Society 107. Philadelphia. 471–472.

Fischer, Loren R., and Knutson, F. Brent. 1969. "An Enthronement Ritual at Ugarit." *Journal of Near Eastern Studies* 28: 157–167.

Flusser, D. 1971. "Seventy Shepherds, Vision of." *Encyclopedia Judaica* 14: 1198–1199.

Ford, J. Massyngberde. 1979. "Jewish Law and Animal Symbolism." *Journal for the Study of Judaism* 10: 203–212.

Frankfort, Henri. 1978. *Kingship and the Gods*. Chicago and London.

Frye, Northrop. 1957. *Anatomy of Criticism*. Princeton, New Jersey.

Funk, R. W. 1966. *Language, Hermeneutic, and Word of God*. New York.

Gaston, Lloyd. 1970. *No Stone on Another*. Leiden.

Genge, H. 1971. "Zum 'Lebensbaum' in den Keilschriftkulturen." *Acta Orientalia* 33: 321–334.

Ginsberg, H. L. 1935. "The Victory of the Land-God over the Sea-God." *Journal of the Palestinian Oriental Society* 15: 327–333.

— 1948. *Studies in Daniel*. Texts and Studies of the Jewish Theological Seminary of America 14. New York.

Ginzberg, L. 1909–1955. *The Legends of the Jews*. 7 vols. Philadelphia.

Goetze, A. 1947. "Historical Allusions in Old Babylonian Omen Texts." *Journal of Cuneiform Studies* 1: 253–265.

Gowan, Donald E. 1977. "The Exile in Jewish Apocalyptic." In *Scripture in History and Theology*. Essays in Honor of J. Coert Rylaarsdam. Edited by Arthur L. Merrill and Thomas W. Overholt. Pittsburgh, Pennsylvania. 205–219.

Grayson, A. K., and Lambert, W. G. 1964. "Akkadian Prophecies." *Journal of Cuneiform Studies* 18: 7–30.

Grayson, A. K. 1975. *Babylonian Historical-Literary Texts*. Toronto-Buffalo.

Griffiths, J. Gwyn. 1983. "Apocalyptic in the Hellenistic Era." In *Apocalypticism in the Mediterranean World and the Near East*: Proceedings of the International Colloquium on Apocalypticism, Uppsala. August 12–17, 1979. Edited by David Hellholm. Tübingen. 273–293.

Gunkel, Hermann. 1895. *Schöpfung und Chaos in Urzeit und Endzeit*. Göttingen.

Gunneweg, A. H. J. 1964. "Ueber den Sitz im Leben der sog. Stammessprüche." *Zeitschrift für die Alttestamentliche Wissenschaft* 76: 245–255.

Hallo, W. W. 1966. "Accadian Apocalypses." *Israel Exploration Journal* 16: 231–242.

Hambly, Wilfred Dyson. 1937. *Source Book for African Anthropology*. Field Museum of Natural History 26. 2 vols. Chicago.

Hammershaimb, E. 1960. "On the Ethics of the Old Testament Prophets." In *Supplements to Vetus Testamentum 7*. Leiden. 75–93.

Hanson, Paul D. 1975. *The Dawn of Apocalyptic*. Philadelphia.

— 1976. "Zechariah, Book Of." In *The Interpreter's Dictionary of the Bible*. Supplementary Volume. Edited by K. Crim. Nashville. 982–983.

Hartman, Louis F., and Di Lella, A. 1978. *The Book of Daniel*. Garden City, New York.

Hawkes, Terence, 1972. *Metaphor*. The Critical Idiom 25. Edited by John D. Jump. London.

Hengel, Martin. 1974. *Judaism and Hellenism*. 2 vols. London.

Herzfeld, Ernst. 1947. *Zoroaster and His World*. 2 vols. Princeton.

Hooker, Morna. 1967. *The Son of Man in Mark*. London.

Houghton, William. 1863. "Unicorn." In *A Dictionary of the Bible*. Edited by William Smith. Vol. 3. London. 1595–1596.

Howe, James. 1977. "Carrying the Village: Cuna Political Metaphors." In *The Social Use of Metaphor*. Edited by J. David Sapir and J. Christopher Crocker. Philadelphia. 132–163.

Hultgård, Anders. 1977. *L'eschatologie des Testaments des Douze Patriarches*. Vol. 1. Interprétation des textes. Uppsala.

— 1980. "The Ideal 'Levite', the Davidic Messiah, and the Saviour Priest in the Testaments of the Twelve Patriarchs." In *Ideal Figures in Ancient Judaism*. Edited by George W. E.

Nickelsburg and John J. Collins. Michigan. 93–110.

Janssen, J. M. A. 1954. "Over Farao Bocchoris." In *Varia Historica aangeboden aan Professor Doctor A. W. Byvanck*. Assen. 17–29.

Jastrow, Morris. 1914. *Babylonian-Assyrian Birth Omens and Their Cultural Significance*. Giessen.

Jeremias, Christian. 1977. *Die Nachtgesichte des Sacharja*. Göttingen.

Jeremias, Joachim. 1966. "Das Lamm, das aus der Jungfrau hervorging." *Zeitschrift für die Neutestamentliche Wissenschaft* 57: 216–219.

— 1968. "ποιμήν." *Theological Dictionary of the New Testament 6*. Edited by G. Kittel and G. Friedrich. Grand Rapids. 485–502.

— 1971. *New Testament Theology*. Vol. 1. London.

Jonge, M. de. 1971. "Recent Studies on the Testaments of the Twelve Patriarchs." *Svensk exegetisk Årsbok* 36: 77–96.

— 1975. *Studies on the Testaments of the Twelve Patriarchs: Text and Interpretation*. Studia in Veteris Testamenti Pseudepigrapha 3. Leiden.

Junker, Hubert. 1932. *Untersuchungen über literarische und exegetische Probleme des Buches Daniel*. Bonn.

Kákosy, L. 1966. "Prophecies of Ram Gods." *Acta Orientalia* 19: 344–345.

Klauck, H.-J. 1978. *Allegorie und Allegorese in Synoptischen Gleichnistexten*. Münster.

Klein, Jacob. 1968. "Šulgi D: A Neo-Sumerian Royal Hymn." Ph.D. dissertation. University of Pennsylvania.

Knibb, Michael A. 1976. "The Exile in the Literature of the Intertestamental Period." *The Heythrop Journal* 17: 253–272.

— 1978. *The Ethiopic Book of Enoch*. In consultation with Edward Ullendorff. 2 vols. Oxford.

— 1982. "Prophecy and the emergence of the Jewish apocalypses." In *Israel's Prophetic Tradition*. Essays in Honour of Peter R. Ackroyd. Cambridge. 155–180.

Koch, Klaus. 1961. "Spätisraelitisches Geschichtsdenken am Beispiel des Buches Daniel." *Historische Zeitschrift* 193: 1–32.

— 1966a. "Das Lamm, das Ägypten vernichtet." *Zeitschrift für die Neutestamentliche Wissenschaft* 57: 79–93.

— 1966b. "Die Apokalyptik und ihre Zukunftserwartungen." In *Kontexte 3: Die Zeit Jesu*. Edited by Hans-Jürgen Schultz. Stuttgart and Berlin. 51–58.

— 1972. *The Rediscovery of Apocalyptic*. London.

— 1980. *Das Buch Daniel*. Darmstadt.

— 1983. "Vom profetischen zum apokalyptischen Visionsbericht." In *Apocalypticism in the Mediterranean World and the Near East*: Proceedings of the International Colloquium on Apocalypticism, Uppsala. August 12–17, 1979. Edited by David Hellholm. Tübingen. 413–446.

Kraeling, Emil G. H. 1933. "Some Babylonian and Iranian Mythology in the Seventh Chapter of Daniel." In *Oriental Studies in Honour of Cursetji Erachji Pavry*. Edited by Jal Dastur Cursetji Pavry. London. 228–231.

Krall, J. 1898. "Vom König Bokchoris." In *Festgaben zu ehren Max Büdinger's*. Innsbruck. 3–11.

Kraus, H.-J. 1972. *Psalmen 2*. Biblischer Kommentar. Altes Testament. Berlin.

Lacocque, André. 1979. *The Book of Daniel*. Translated by David Pallauer. Revised English Edition. Atlanta, Georgia.

Lambert, W. G. 1960. *Babylonian Wisdom Literature*. Oxford.

— 1978. *The Background of Jewish Apocalyptic*. London.

Lang, Andrew; Leaf, Walter; and Myers, Ernest, translators. n.d. *The Iliad of Homer*. New York.

Leichty, Erle. 1970. *The Omen Series Šumma izbu*. Locust Valley, New York.

Lengerke, Caesar von. 1835. *Das Buch Daniel*. Königsberg.

Lenglet, A. 1972. "La structure littéraire de Daniel 2–7". *Biblica* 53: 169–190.

Luckenbill, Daniel D. 1927. *Ancient Records of Assyria*. 2 vols. Chicago.

Mason, Rex A. 1976. "The Relation of Zech 9–14 to Proto-Zechariah." *Zeitschrift für die Alttestamentliche Wissenschaft* 88: 227–238.

McCown, C. C. 1925. "Hebrew and Egyptian Apocalyptic Literature." *Harvard Theological Review* 18: 357–411.

Meyer, Eduard. 1909. "Ein neues Bruchstück Manethos über das Lamm des Bokchoris." *Zeitschrift für Ägyptische Sprache und Altertumskunde* 45: 135–136.

Milik, J. T., ed. 1976. *The Books of Enoch*: Aramaic fragments of Qumran Cave 4. With the collaboration of Matthew Black. Oxford.

Miller, Patrick D. 1967. "El the Warrior." *Harvard Theological Review* 60: 411–431.

— 1971. "Animal Names as Designations in Ugaritic and Hebrew." *Ugaritische Forschungen* 2: 177–186.

— 1973. *The Divine Warrior in Early Israel*. Harvard Semitic Monographs 5. Cambridge, Mass.

Moortgat, A. 1949. *Tammuz*. Berlin.

Müller, Dieter. 1961. "Der gute Hirte." *Zeitschrift für Ägyptische Sprache und Altertumskunde* 86: 126–143.

Müller, Hans-Peter. 1972. "Mantische Weisheit und Apokalyptik." In *Supplements to Vetus Testamentum* 22. Leiden.

Muilenburg, James. 1956. "The Book of Isaiah, Chapters 40–66, Introduction and Exegesis." In *The Interpreter's Bible*. Vol. 5. New York. 381–773.

Nagel, W. 1964. *Die Bauern- und Stadtkulturen im vordynastischen Vorderasien*. Berlin.

Nickelsburg, George W. E. 1972. *Resurrection, Immortality, and Eternal Life in Intertestamental Judaism*. Harvard Theological Studies 26. Cambridge, Mass.

North, C. R. 1952. *Isaiah 40–55—Introduction and a Commentary*. Torch Bible Commentaries. London.

Noth, Martin. 1966. *The Laws in the Pentateuch and other studies*. Translated by D. R. Ap-Thomas. Edinburgh and London.

Oppenheim, A. Leo. 1959. "On an Operational Device in Mesopotamian Bureaucracy." *Journal of Near Eastern Studies* 18: 121–128.

Ortony, Andrew. 1979. "Metaphor: A Multidimensional Problem." In *Metaphor and Thought*. Edited by A. Ortony. Cambridge. 1–18.

Parrot, A. 1962. *Sumer*. 2nd ed. München.

Pepper, Stephen C. 1942. *World Hypotheses*. Berkeley and Los Angeles.

Perrin, Norman. 1974. "Eschatology and Hermeneutics: Reflections on Method in the Interpretation of the New Testament." *Journal of Biblical Literature* 93: 3–14.

— 1976. *Jesus and the Language of the Kingdom*. London.

Pinches, T. G. 1908. *The Old Testament in the Light of Historical Records and Legends of Assyria and Babylonia*. London.

Plöger, Otto. 1965. *Das Buch Daniel*. Kommentar zum Alten Testament 18. Gütersloh.

Plot, Robert P. 1677. *The Natural History of Oxfordshire, Being an Essay toward the Natural History of England*. Oxford.

Porteous, Norman. 1979. *Daniel*. 2nd. ed. London.

Porter, F. C. 1905. *The Messages of the Apocalyptical Writers*. New York.

Postgate, J. N. 1975. "Some Old Babylonian Shepherds and Their Flocks." *Journal of Semitic Studies* 20: 1–21.

Pritchard, James B., ed. 1950. *Ancient Near Eastern Texts Relating to the Old Testament*.

Princeton, New Jersey.

— 1969. *Ancient Near Eastern Texts Relating to the Old Testament*. 3rd. ed. Princeton, New Jersey.

Rad, Gerhard von. 1965. *Old Testament Theology*. 2 vols. London.

Reiner, E. 1974. "New Light on Some Historical Omens." In *Anatolian Studies Presented to Hans Gustav Güterbock on the Occasion of His 65th Birthday*. Edited by K. Bittel, P. H. J. Houwink ten Cate, and E. Reiner. Istanbul. 257–261.

Reisman, Daniel. 1969. "Two Neo-Sumerian Royal Hymns." Ph.D. dissertation. University of Pennsylvania.

Richards, I. A. 1936. *The Philosophy of Rhetoric*. Oxford.

Ricoeur, Paul. 1975. "Biblical Hermeneutics." *Semeia* 4: 27–148.

— 1978. *The Rule of Metaphor*. London.

— 1979. "Foreword." In A. Lacocque, *The Book of Daniel*. Atlanta. xvii–xxvi.

Rimbach, James A. 1978. "Critical Notes: Bears or Bees? Sefire I A 31 and Daniel 7." *Journal of Biblical Literature* 97: 565–566.

Ringgren, Helmer. 1983. "Akkadian Apocalypses." In *Apocalypticism in the Mediterranean World and the Near East*: Proceedings of the International Colloquium on Apocalypticism, Uppsala. August 12–17, 1979. Edited by David Hellholm. Tübingen. 379–386.

Rowley, H. H. 1944. *The Relevance of Apocalyptic*. London and Redhill.

Sahlin, Harald. 1969. "Antiochus IV. Epiphanes und Judas Makkabäus." *Studia Theologica* 23: 41–68.

Salo, Vello. 1968. "Joseph, Sohn der Färse." *Biblische Zeitschrift* 12: 94–95.

Sapir, J. David. 1977. "The Anatomy of Metaphor." In *The Social Use of Metaphor*. Edited by J. David Sapir and J. Christopher Crocker. Philadelphia.

Scholfield, A. F., translator. 1959. *Aelian: On the Characteristics of Animals*. Loeb Classical Library. Cambridge, Mass. and London.

Schrader, E., ed. 1889–1915. *Keilinschriftliche Bibliothek*. Sammlung von assyrischen und babylonischen Texten. 6 vols. Berlin.

Schrenk, Gottlob. 1965. "τὸ ἱερόν." *Theological Dictionary of the New Testament* 3. Edited by G. Kittel and G. Friedrich. Grand Rapids. 230–247.

Seibert, Ilse. 1969. *Hirt-Herde-König*: Zur Herausbildung des Königtums in Mesopotamien. Berlin.

Sjöberg, Åke W.; Bergmann, E.; and Gragg, Gene B. 1969. *The Collection of the Sumerian Temple Hymns*. Locust Valley, New York.

Staub, Urs. 1978. "Das Tier mit den Hörnen." *Freiburger Zeitschrift für Philosophie und Theologie* 25: 351–397.

Steck, Odil Hannes. 1967. *Israel und das gewaltsame Geschick der Propheten*. Wissenschaftliche Monographien zum Alten und Neuen Testament. Neukirchen-Vluyn.

— 1980. "Weltgeschehen und Gottesvolk im Buche Daniel." In *Kirche*. Festschrift für Günther Bornkamm zum 75. Geburtstag. Edited by Dieter Lührmann and Georg Strecker. Tübingen. 53–77.

Stephan, Stephan H. 1925. "Animals in Palestinian Folklore." *The Journal of the Palestine Oriental Society* 5: 92–155.

Stern, M. 1961. "The Relations between Judea and Rome during the Rule of John Hyrcanus." *Zion* 26: 1–22.

Stolz, Fritz. 1972. "Die Bäume des Gottesgartens auf dem Libanon." *Zeitschrift für die Alttestamentliche Wissenschaft* 84: 141–156.

Stone, Michael E. 1975. *The Armenian Version of the Testament of Joseph*. Missoula, Montana.

Te Selle, S. 1975. *Speaking in Parables*: A Study in Metaphor and Theology. Philadelphia.

Torrey, Charles Cutler. 1954. "Alexander Jannaeus and the Archangel Michael." *Vetus Testamentum* 4: 208–211.

Turner, Victor. 1974. *Dramas, Fields and Metaphors*: Symbolic Action in Human Society. Ithaca and London.

Tyler, Stephen A. 1969. *Cognitive Anthropology*. New York.

Vancil, Jack W. 1975. "The Symbolism of the Shepherd in Biblical, Intertestamental, and New Testament Material." Ph.D. dissertation. Dropsie University.

Via, D. O. 1967. *The Parables*: Their Literary and Existential Dimension. Philadelphia.

Volz, P. 1934. *Die Eschatologie der jüdischen Gemeinde im neutestamentlichen Zeitalter nach den Quellen der rabbinischen, apokalyptischen und apokryphen Literatur dargestellt.* Tübingen.

Weder, H. 1978. *Die Gleichnisse Jesu als Metaphern*. Göttingen.

Weidner, Ernst. 1967. *Gestirn-Darstellungen auf Babylonischen Tontafeln*. Österreichische Akademie der Wissenschaften. Philosophisch-Historische Klasse. 254/2. Wien.

Wheelwright, Philip. 1954. *The Burning Fountain*. Bloomington, Indiana.

— 1962. *Metaphor and Reality*. Bloomington, Indiana.

Wilder, A. 1964. *Early Christian Rhetoric*: The Language of the Gospel. New York.

Wiseman, D. J. 1952. "A New Stela of Aššur-Naṣir-Pal II." *Iraq* 14: 24–30.

Wittstruck, Thorne. 1978. "The Influence of Treaty Curse Imagery on the Beast Imagery of Daniel 7." *Journal of Biblical Literature* 97: 100–102.

Witzel, M. 1935. *Tammuz-Liturgien und Verwandtes*. Analecta Orientalia 10. Rome.

Zeitlin, Solomon. 1961–1962. "Queen Salome and King Jannaeus Alexander." *Jewish Quarterly Review* 51: 1–33.

Zimmerli, Walther. 1969. *Ezechiel*. Biblischer Kommentar. Altes Testament. Neukirchen-Vluyn.

— 1976. "Alttestamentliche Prophetie und Apokalyptik auf dem Wege zur 'Rechtfertigung des Gottlosen.'" In *Rechtfertigung*. Festschrift für Ernst Käsemann zum 70. Geburtstag. Edited by Johannes Friedrich, Wolfgang Pöhlmann and Peter Stuhlmacher. Tübingen and Göttingen. 575–592.

Zimmern, H. apud Schrader, E. 1903. *Die Keilinschriften und das Alte Testament*. 3rd. ed. Berlin.